Desperate
Dependency

Desperate
Dependency

Finding Christ Relevant
to Every Area of Life

J. KIRK & MELANIE D. LEWIS

REDEMPTION
PRESS

© 2011 Cover design by Bill Taylor.

Bill offers these thoughts behind the creation of his cover design: Out of the chaos of the world we live in (background painting) you can find the help and comfort we all desperately seek (hand with cross image), and the pages in this book can be a guide to finding the peace that only Christ can give (hand is also in the shape of a dove with olive branch and the red in painting signifies the blood of Christ which covers our sins).

ISBN 13: 978-1-63232-700-0 (Print)
        978-1-63232-701-7 (ePub)
        978-1-63232-702-4 (Mobi)

Library of Congress Catalog Card Number: 2010909718

To the countless people who have shared their lives with us.
Thank you for helping us learn to be desperately dependent.

O magnify the LORD with me, and let us exalt his name together.

—Ps. 34:3 KJV

Contents

Introduction

WHEN YOU LOOK around, and perhaps if you look within, you can easily find people who seem desperate as they depend on a variety of creative solutions to experience satisfaction and fill the void in their hearts. Unfortunately, even Christians fail to recognize God's design of a relationship that is desperately dependent on Jesus to complete their lives. *Desperate Dependency* identifies the deceptions and points the searching soul to find Christ relevant to the intricacies of life's problems and pain. As you submit to His purpose of transforming you into the image of Christ, you will experience His promised fruit, including love, joy, and peace.

Throughout these pages we have incorporated biblical principles to challenge you to a relevant relationship with Jesus. Please do not give in to the temptation to skim or skip over the Scripture passages that are included. The verses referenced are God's words directed to you because He desires your selfish sin nature to be confronted by the Holy Spirit's conviction in your life so that you can live in complete dependence on Christ. Connect with His Spirit while working through the Insight Journal exercises. Communicate with God through the Psalms Prayer Patterns. Take this time to grow in your dependence on Him.

This book is not a compilation of our ideas that we asked God to bless, but rather it is a documentation of God's working in our lives as we have realized our inability and God's capabilities. We have struggled and prayed for God to work in us so that we might in turn share with you how He wants to work in your life. In conveying His heart to you we have become desperately dependent.

What difference is there in your life because you say you are a Christian? Have you realized that you cannot successfully live independently from Jesus? Have you discovered His divine enablement that produces personal empowerment? Christ wants to be relevant to every area of your life. Will you let Him? Will you be desperately dependent?

I waited patiently for the Lord to help me,
 and he turned to me and heard my cry.
He lifted me out of the pit of despair,
 out of the mud and the mire.
He set my feet on solid ground
 and steadied me as I walked along.
He has given me a new song to sing,
 a hymn of praise to our God.
Many will see what he has done and be amazed.
 They will put their trust in the Lord.

Oh, the joys of those who trust the Lord,
 who have no confidence in the proud
 or in those who worship idols.
O Lord my God, you have performed many wonders for us.
 Your plans for us are too numerous to list.
 You have no equal.
If I tried to recite all your wonderful deeds,
 I would never come to the end of them.

You take no delight in sacrifices or offerings.
 Now that you have made me listen, I finally understand—
 you don't require burnt offerings or sin offerings.
Then I said, "Look, I have come.
 As is written about me in the Scriptures:
I take joy in doing your will, my God,
 for your instructions are written on my heart."

I have told all your people about your justice.
    I have not been afraid to speak out,
        as you, O LORD, well know.
I have not kept the good news of your justice hidden in my heart;
    I have talked about your faithfulness and saving power.
I have told everyone in the great assembly
    of your unfailing love and faithfulness.

LORD, don't hold back your tender mercies from me.
    Let your unfailing love and faithfulness always protect me.
For troubles surround me—
    too many to count!
My sins pile up so high
    I can't see my way out.
They outnumber the hairs on my head.
    I have lost all courage.

Please, LORD, rescue me!
    Come quickly, LORD, and help me.
May those who try to destroy me
    be humiliated and put to shame.
May those who take delight in my trouble
    be turned back in disgrace.
Let them be horrified by their shame,
    for they said, "Aha! We've got him now!"

But may all who search for you
    be filled with joy and gladness in you.
May those who love your salvation
    repeatedly shout, "The LORD is great!"
As for me, since I am poor and needy,
    let the Lord keep me in his thoughts.
You are my helper and my savior.
    O my God, do not delay.

—Ps. 40:1–17

PART 1

The Problem—Christ Is Missing

CHAPTER 1

What's Missing?

IN OUR EARLY years of school we were handed a delightful picture to evaluate. "Look at the picture and figure out what is missing," we were told. Carefully we pondered each detail and compared it in our minds with a similar image we had seen before. Some of the pictures were ridiculously obvious in their omissions, but others were painfully elusive. It was terribly frustrating when our classmates would bounce in their seats and exclaim, "I know! I know! I know!" while we continued our search. We would view the picture from side to side, top to bottom, over and over again. What a relief when we could finally notice the missing piece.

Then the teacher's next instructions followed: "Now draw in the missing part." When it came to drawing, I (Melanie) was definitely not labeled as talented! I would struggle and agonize in my attempts to fill in the missing piece. Needless to say, it was always obvious where I had filled in the missing lines. Surprisingly, I could always tell where the talented children had drawn their lines too. Since none of us were the original artist of the drawing, we could not perfectly complete the picture.

We Are Incomplete

Unfortunately, as adults there are some lessons we still have not learned from that elementary school exercise. Our lives are given to us as a wonderful design. We were created carefully and meticulously for a marvelous purpose. Each day we evaluate and ponder the intricate details of the many aspects that come together to structure our lives. Repeatedly we come to the conclusion that something is missing. We struggle in our search as others around us exclaim, "I know! I know! I know!" and lead us on one fruitless chase after another. In an attempt to not appear stupid, we create our own design to fill in the emptiness. But no matter how creative we are, our ultimate creation never matches the design our Creator planned unless we allow Him to complete the picture.

God is the Master Designer. In His mind's eye He can see the completed masterpiece of our lives. The vastness of the task does not overwhelm Him. He delights in His creation. Knowing from the beginning to the ending His desired results, He patiently fashions the portrait. It is His self-portrait.

Unfortunately, the design we are sketching is our self-portrait. We are looking for happiness, fulfillment, meaning, control, freedom, belonging, relationships, money, contentment, satisfaction, and the list could go on and on. Foolishly we attempt to complete what the Master designed. Disappointment results when a novice attempts to complete a masterpiece independent of the Master.

God's design requires us to be dependent on Him. Because we believe Satan's lie that we are capable on our own, we seek to fill the void to our own satisfaction. All the while God replies, "I know!" He patiently waits for us to come to the Master Designer for our picture to be perfectly complete. "So you also are complete through your union with Christ" (Col. 2:10).

We Are Trying to Complete Ourselves

Consider these two questions: What do I really want? How will I attain it? Apart from a relevant relationship with Jesus Christ we will look to people, positions, and possessions to empower and complete our lives. The sin nature motivates us to be desperate individuals, and we choose influences other than Christ.

Consider the following examples:

Some time later, the LORD spoke to Abram in a vision and said to him, "Do not be afraid, Abram, for I will protect you, and your reward will be great."

But Abram replied, "O Sovereign LORD, what good are all your blessings when I don't even have a son? Since you've given me no children, Eliezer of Damascus, a servant in my household, will inherit all my wealth. You have given me no descendants of my own, so one of my servants will be my heir."

Then the LORD said to him, "No, your servant will not be your heir, for you will have a son of your own who will be your heir." Then the LORD took Abram outside and said to him, "Look up into the sky and count the stars if you can. That's how many descendants you will have!"

—Gen. 15:1–5

Now Sarai, Abram's wife, had not been able to bear children for him. But she had an Egyptian servant named Hagar. So Sarai said to Abram, "The LORD has prevented me from having children. Go and sleep with my servant. Perhaps I can have children through her." And Abram agreed with Sarai's proposal. So Sarai, Abram's wife, took Hagar the Egyptian servant and gave her to Abram as a wife. (This happened ten years after Abram had settled in the land of Canaan.)

—Gen. 16:1–3

Diane felt out of control in her life. When she met George she knew he was the answer to all her problems. He was a very successful businessman with many people in his employment. After twenty years with the same company, he knew exactly how things needed to be done and how to make sure they got done exactly the way they needed to be done. The employees knew George had a solution to every problem and could tell them step by step how to accomplish the necessary task. His excellence in leadership had been awarded frequently.

Since George was so accustomed to running things in an orderly fashion at work, he shared his expertise with Diane all the time. "He says I do a wonderful job preparing the meals he likes, but I need to learn a little more about using spices. Yesterday I received a special lesson on folding the bath towels correctly. If I miss a weed in the flowerbeds, he is sure to show me exactly where it is. He continuously reminds me that if I just follow his instructions everything will run smoothly. I just don't know what I would do without him, but there are some times when I would sure like to find out." Diane did not have the solution for the frustration, anger, turmoil, and rejection she felt.

The ladder of success possessed a mesmerizing appeal for Howard. His definition of success was having enough money. Enough to buy the cars he wanted. Enough to live in a house in a prestigious neighborhood. Enough to enable his children to attend the most elite schools. Enough to purchase the clothes that identified his family as upper class. Enough to be able to do what he wanted when he wanted. Enough to make people stand in awe and be jealous of what he attained. Enough.

Howard followed one promising proposal after another. His computer continuously relayed more enticing opportunities. He was proficient in every investment strategy. Pages were added to his portfolio daily. But even with all he attained, it was never enough. Anxiety plagued him. Discouragement hounded him. Lust continuously tempted him.

Angie had attained her goal. They had moved into the perfect house in the perfect subdivision, and she was going to make sure everything stayed perfect. Her floors were polished with a perfect shine. The walls were painted with designer paint. The baseboards were repainted every time a scuff appeared. The children were delighted that they were not allowed to wear their shoes in the house, but not so delighted that they were only allowed to have one toy out of its designated location at a time. Their yard was meticulously manicured, with every pebble in place, and not a dandelion to be found. Angie was convinced her house was the evidence she was in right standing with God. After all, look at how He had blessed her! Her house gave her a sense of worth and value.

But then the tornado came. Within a few brief moments everything was lost, except the family's lives. And even more devastating was the fact that the insurance company did not reimburse for losses occurring as a result of "acts of God." Why had God left her with unhappiness, despair, disappointment, and jealousy?

Could you identify with any of the previous examples? In each of the illustrations individuals were attempting to complete their lives by their own design. They searched for satisfaction that was fleeting by employing methods they could control. But ask yourself this question: "Am I trying to complete my life by my own means?"

- Do I gravitate to *people* to search for satisfaction?
- Do I use *positions* (CEO, wife, husband, mother, millionaire) to seek fulfillment?
- Do I believe *possessions* can produce significance?

Consider it this way: *Who or what can I not live without?* Your response reveals what empowers your life.

We Can Only Be Complete in Christ

We fall into a trap if we believe a person, position, or possession other than Jesus can complete our lives. In our daily struggles we search for ways to stimulate our emotions or sedate our emotions in order to feel good. But that which makes me feel good enslaves me. The end result is bondage. What a cunning ploy Satan has devised! "This is what you need to feel good about yourself," he asserts as he lays the net to ensnare you. "There is a way that seems right to a man, but in the end it leads to death" (Prov. 14:12; 16:25 NIV). "An evil man is held captive by his own sins; they are ropes that catch and hold him" (Prov. 5:22). These strongholds are fortifications that keep us imprisoned.

But if you really want something, who is going to stop you? The natural desire of the heart is self-indulgence: I want what I want! The end of all self-indulgence is bondage. The very thing we want will destroy us. "Temptation comes from our own desires, which entice us and drag us away. These desires give birth to sinful actions. And when sin is allowed to grow, it gives birth to death" (James 1:14–15). Our self-centered choices lead to strongholds that result in relationship problems, emotional difficulties, physical challenges, and even a crisis of faith. And so we sit, looking at life through the portholes of our own strongholds that have imprisoned us.

The Galatians were struggling with similar issues. Paul poses this question to them: "After starting your Christian lives in the Spirit, why are you now trying to become perfect by your own human effort?" (Gal. 3:3). They had fallen into the deception that by practicing religious rites they could be made right with God. They had arrived at the solution that a relationship with Christ was not enough; they needed more. Paul pleads with them: "So Christ has truly set us free. Now make sure that you stay free, and don't get tied up again in slavery to the law" (Gal. 5:1).

In Paul's writing to Timothy he admonished Timothy to point people to the truth, so "Then they will come to their senses and escape from the devil's trap. For they have been held captive by him to do whatever he wants" (2 Tim. 2:26).

If we live within God's parameters, we will live in freedom. Mistakenly we believe that freedom is living without rules. With this definition you may choose to live in freedom while driving down the road disregarding speed limits, traffic lights, and dividing lines. Before arriving at your destination, you will likely be in an accident and injure yourself or someone else, receive a ticket, or be jailed. Dr. James Dobson has repeatedly claimed that children raised without boundaries grow to be insecure.

Years ago, during the early days of the progressive-education movement, an enthusiastic theorist decided to take down the chain-link fence that surrounded the nursery-school yard. He thought the children would feel more freedom of movement without that visible barrier surrounding them. When the fence was removed, however, the boys and girls huddled near the center of the play yard. Not only did they not wander away; they didn't even venture to the edge of the grounds. Clearly, there is a security for all of us in defined boundaries.[1]

So if people, positions, or possessions do not offer freedom or the solution for enjoying a complete life, what is the solution? Galatians 5:16 (NIV) supplies the answer: "So I say, live by the Spirit, and you will not gratify the desires of the sinful nature." We are to conduct our lives "by the Spirit." This requires a relationship with God's Spirit in which we dependently trust Him with all our needs. This is an astonishing assertion, "…you will not carry out the desire of the flesh" (NASB). In the Greek text the double negative construction emphasizes, "there is no way on earth, you can ever" carry out the desires of the flesh if you are living by the Spirit. Do you like the sound of that? The catch is that brokenness is a prerequisite: we cannot depend on God without first giving up our willfulness. We must give up the right to want what we want and trade it for wanting what God wants. "But I don't want to give up what I want," you may whine. Then you are not ready for a desperately dependent relationship on God that results in a life that is divinely enabled. This relationship begins by giving up our self-centered lives in exchange for Christ-centered lives that result from the forgiveness of sin. Without giving up our willfulness, we cannot know the heart of God and want what He wants.

If we are to be a picture of Christ, a Christian, then we are to live as He lived—desperately dependent on God for divine enablement for personal empowerment. Thus, holiness is true healthiness—to be complete in Christ. How is this possible? We tear down strongholds through obedience to Christ. "We use God's mighty weapons, not worldly weapons, to knock down the strongholds of human reasoning and to destroy false arguments. We destroy every proud obstacle that keeps people from knowing God. We capture their rebellious thoughts and teach them to obey Christ" (2 Cor. 10:4–5).

Through our obedience, that special place where divine enablement meets with personal empowerment, we are doing what God says for us to do. Although the spirit of self will fight the Spirit of God, when our minds are filled with His words and with our interaction through prayer, we will access the power of God. "For you have been called to live in freedom, my brothers and sisters. But don't use your freedom to satisfy your sinful nature" (Gal. 5:13).

So I say, let the Holy Spirit guide your lives. Then you won't be doing what your sinful nature craves. The sinful nature wants to do evil, which is just the opposite of what the Spirit wants. And the Spirit gives us desires that are the opposite of what the sinful nature desires. These two forces are constantly fighting each other, so you are not free to carry out your good intentions. But when the Spirit directs you, you are not under obligation to the law of Moses.

When you follow the desires of your sinful nature, the results are very clear: sexual immorality, impurity, lustful pleasures, idolatry, sorcery, hostility, quarreling, jealousy, outbursts of anger, selfish ambition, dissension, division, envy, drunkenness, wild parties, and other sins like these. Let me tell you again, as I have before, that anyone living that sort of life will not inherit the Kingdom of God.

But the Holy Spirit produces this kind of fruit in our lives: love, joy, peace, patience, kindness, goodness, faithfulness, gentleness, and self-control. There is no law against these things!

Those who belong to Christ Jesus have nailed the passions and desires of their sinful nature to his cross and crucified them there. Since we are living by the Spirit, let us follow the Spirit's leading in every part of our lives.

—Gal. 5:16–25

God wants me to be complete in the person of Christ, in my position as His child, and in the possession of His righteousness. But, we say, I have my own life plan that I am sure will be exactly what God wants for me, so if He would just enable me to accomplish my purposes I could be complete. I want God to empower me to not need Him. And so we travel our own path, claiming to be a Christian but refusing to be desperately dependent on Christ, who offers His portrait in place of our sketch.

Shirley was empowered in her job working as a human resource officer for a prominent company. Her husband was a local celebrity. She enjoyed all the food she wanted. Life was good. Until her husband left her for another woman, and she lost her job as a result of medical complications that were exacerbated by her obesity. This is how she tells her story.

I used to live my life waiting to find a way to beat the system. (God was the system.) I didn't ask for much. I just wanted to be able to sin and get away with it. But sin has a way of eating at your heart with a silence so deadly you sometimes don't even know it's happening until you are almost consumed.

That was me. After hundreds of attempts to lose weight and control my life, I thought I would get my weight problem under control and come to feel better about myself and then everything would be peachy-keen.

God had other plans. He planned to rescue me from Egypt. That all sounded well and good, but I had no idea that between the good old hometown of Egypt and the wonderful Promised Land that I longed for, was a scorching hot, almost unbearable desert.

I remained there for a long, long time with nothing in sight but more desert. God took that opportunity to hold a mirror before me so I could come to see the depth of my sinfulness for the very first time. You see, I thought it was just a weight problem, and maybe I just needed some self-esteem. But God began to reveal to my heart that my problem was that I was living in complete deception and had been my whole life.

I guess we all spend some time on the edge. I've sort of lived my life there. I kept thinking that I could always change later. But God brought me to the end of myself and I was completely sickened by what I saw. It was the first time in my life that I could not find anything in that mirror but a reflection of filthy rags. What a horrifying moment that was for my self-centered heart. And what a liberating moment it was as God accepted me right where I was, asking nothing but that I put my complete trust in Him.

Somewhere along the line I started to long for Jesus more than I was afraid of losing control of the food. He had proven Himself faithful, and I began to trust this God that I used to fear with all my heart. At the point I finally gave it up and left it at the foot of the cross, I couldn't find any words to say except, "God, save me from me." I hold on to the hope found in Christ Jesus alone. May God continue to save me from myself.

In the book of Isaiah we read stories of how God repeatedly invited His children to trust Him. Chapter 30 elaborates on some of the results.

"What sorrow awaits my rebellious children,"
     says the LORD.
"You make plans that are contrary to mine.
     You make alliances not directed by my Spirit,
     thus piling up your sins.
For without consulting me,
     you have gone down to Egypt for help.
You have put your trust in Pharaoh's protection.
     You have tried to hide in his shade.

But by trusting Pharaoh, you will be humiliated,
    and by depending on him, you will be disgraced.
For though his power extends to Zoan
    and his officials have arrived in Hanes,
all who trust in him will be ashamed.
    He will not help you.
    Instead, he will disgrace you."

This message came to me concerning the animals in the Negev:

The caravan moves slowly
    across the terrible desert to Egypt—
donkeys weighed down with riches
    and camels loaded with treasure—
    all to pay for Egypt's protection.
They travel through the wilderness,
    a place of lionesses and lions,
    a place where vipers and poisonous snakes live.
All this, and Egypt will give you nothing in return.
    Egypt's promises are worthless!
Therefore, I call her Rahab—
    the Harmless Dragon.

Now go and write down these words.
    Write them in a book.
They will stand until the end of time
    as a witness
that these people are stubborn rebels
    who refuse to pay attention to the LORD's instructions.
They tell the seers,
    "Stop seeing visions!"
They tell the prophets,
    "Don't tell us what is right.
Tell us nice things.
    Tell us lies.
Forget all this gloom.

Get off your narrow path.
Stop telling us about your
   'Holy One of Israel.'"

This is the reply of the Holy One of Israel:

"Because you despise what I tell you
   and trust instead in oppression and lies,
calamity will come upon you suddenly—
   like a bulging wall that bursts and falls.
In an instant it will collapse
   and come crashing down.
You will be smashed like a piece of pottery—
   shattered so completely that
there won't be a piece big enough
   to carry coals from a fireplace
   or a little water from the well."

This is what the Sovereign LORD,
   the Holy One of Israel, says:
"Only in returning to me
   and resting in me will you be saved.
In quietness and confidence is your strength.
   But you would have none of it.
You said, 'No, we will get our help from Egypt.
   They will give us swift horses for riding into battle.'
But the only swiftness you are going to see
   is the swiftness of your enemies chasing you!
One of them will chase a thousand of you.
   Five of them will make all of you flee.
You will be left like a lonely flagpole on a hill
   or a tattered banner on a distant mountaintop."

So the LORD must wait for you to come to him
    so he can show you his love and compassion.
For the LORD is a faithful God.
    Blessed are those who wait for his help.

O people of Zion, who live in Jerusalem,
    you will weep no more.
He will be gracious if you ask for help.
    He will surely respond to the sound of your cries.
Though the Lord gave you adversity for food
    and suffering for drink,
he will still be with you to teach you.
    You will see your teacher with your own eyes.
Your own ears will hear him.
    Right behind you a voice will say,
"This is the way you should go,"
    whether to the right or to the left.

—Isa. 30:1–21

By what means are you going to choose to empower your life? Will you allow the Master to complete His self-portrait through your life by means of the fruit of His Spirit? You have the option to choose divine enablement that comes from God to produce personal empowerment in your life. "Those who belong to Christ Jesus have nailed the passions and desires of their sinful nature to his cross and crucified them there. Since we are living by the Spirit, let us follow the Spirit's leading in every part of our lives" (Gal. 5:24–25). If you choose to live by the Spirit, the strongholds will be broken, resulting in a complete, divinely empowered life—a picture of Christ. If you are not dependent on Christ, today is the best day of the rest of your life; it will be downhill from here.

Insight Journal

The Insight Journal questions at the end of each chapter are designed to challenge you to connect with God in a deeper way. Of course, you could quickly move to the next chapter assuming you fully understand what has been presented. But if you take the challenge to assimilate the information more fully, you will discover growth opportunities as the Holy Spirit works to directly apply His truths to your life.

Since there will be five questions at the end of each chapter, you may decide you want to process one question a day as you absorb one chapter per week. You will recognize the Holy Spirit continuing His work in your life as you allow Him to mature you through these truths in your daily experiences.

1. What difference is there in my life because I say I am a Christian? (If you were to come to me and say, "My name is _____ and I am a Christian," what message would you want that to communicate to me?)
2. What's missing in my life?
3. What do I really want? How will I attain what I really want?
4. Who or what can I not live without? Who or what makes me feel alive?
5. Who or what do I turn to when in crisis?

For deeper application, consider how each person in the examples of chapter 1 used people to search for satisfaction, positions to seek fulfillment, and possessions to produce significance.

At the conclusion of each chapter you will find a Psalms Prayer Pattern. These psalms were chosen to provide a model designed by God showing ways we can approach Him in a desperately dependent fashion. Use these Psalms Prayer Patterns to pour out your heart to God while acknowledging your weakness and His strength, as you grow deeper in your relationship with Him.

Psalms Prayer Pattern

O Lord, I give my life to you.
    I trust in you, my God!
Do not let me be disgraced,
    or let my enemies rejoice in my defeat.
No one who trusts in you will ever be disgraced,
    but disgrace comes to those who try to deceive others.

Show me the right path, O Lord;
    point out the road for me to follow.
Lead me by your truth and teach me,
    for you are the God who saves me.
    All day long I put my hope in you.
Remember, O Lord, your compassion and unfailing love,
    which you have shown from long ages past.
Do not remember the rebellious sins of my youth.
    Remember me in the light of your unfailing love,
    for you are merciful, O Lord.

The Lord is good and does what is right;
    he shows the proper path to those who go astray.
He leads the humble in doing right,
    teaching them his way.
The Lord leads with unfailing love and faithfulness
    all who keep his covenant and obey his demands.

For the honor of your name, O LORD,
     forgive my many, many sins.
Who are those who fear the LORD?
     He will show them the path they should choose.
They will live in prosperity,
     and their children will inherit the land.
The LORD is a friend to those who fear him.
     He teaches them his covenant.
My eyes are always on the LORD,
     for he rescues me from the traps of my enemies.

Turn to me and have mercy,
     for I am alone and in deep distress.
My problems go from bad to worse.
     Oh, save me from them all!
Feel my pain and see my trouble.
     Forgive all my sins.
See how many enemies I have
     and how viciously they hate me!
Protect me! Rescue my life from them!
     Do not let me be disgraced, for in you I take refuge.
May integrity and honesty protect me,
     for I put my hope in you.

O God, ransom Israel
     from all its troubles.

—Ps. 25

CHAPTER 2

Am I the Problem?

THE BIBLE TEACHES we can be complete, be fulfilled, possess well-being, and enjoy quality of life only through the person of Jesus Christ as we experience Him as relevant to all areas of our lives. There can be no true happiness or healthiness apart from a desperately dependent connection with Jesus. But with all our wisdom we do not find the solutions for life's struggles in Him. We believe we can be independent. Stop a minute and consider what that word means to you. What are some words that come to your mind when you think of a person being *independent*? Do any of these words match your choices: strong, powerful, complete, confident, self-reliant, or alone? Webster's dictionary definition for *independent* includes "not dependent; not subject to control by others; not affiliated with a larger controlling unit; not requiring or relying on something else; not looking to others for one's opinions or for guidance in conduct; showing a desire for freedom."[1]

On the other hand, consider the word *dependent*. What are some words that come to your mind when you think of a person being *dependent*? Do you come up with mostly negative connotations, such as needy, weak, attached, addicted, or lacking? Webster's dictionary definition for *dependent* includes "determined or conditioned by another; relying on another for support."[2] Especially in our American culture it seems that dependence is discouraged in favor of independence. But we still pride ourselves on the concept that when we are in need we can depend on our fellow Americans to come to our assistance. We live in contradiction, striving for independence we can never actually attain.

I Want to Be Independent

God is the only one who is truly independent, because independence is an attribute of deity. He does not rely on anyone or anything to complete Himself. He is not subject to control by others. Reality sets forth the fact that all that is depends on God. Nothing can exist apart from God. Everything owes its existence to God.

> For through him God created everything
>   in the heavenly realms and on earth.
> He made the things we can see
>   and the things we can't see—
> such as thrones, kingdoms, rulers, and authorities in the unseen world.
>   Everything was created through him and for him.
>
> —Col. 1:16

"But the God of Israel is no idol! / He is the Creator of everything that exists, / including his people, his own special possession. / The Lord of Heaven's Armies is his name!" (Jer. 51:19).

Humanity was designed to be in a dependent relationship. We were never intended to be independent. God's order is for His creation to depend on Him and His sufficiency in all areas of our lives. But we want to be independent.

My (Melanie) garden thrives on neglect. Some people may look at it and say it lives independently, but that is far from the truth. Even my garden needs God to plant, to water, and to give the increase. For my plants to claim independence is arrogant. They would be taking everything for granted. Seeds cannot germinate without soil, water, and sun; and plants even need the bees and worms to do their jobs. But the bees and worms are also interdependent on the process. Without the plants, soil, water, and sun, the creatures could not survive.

For a human to claim, "I can do it myself," is the same as a beautiful plant claiming, "I can do it myself." How absurd.

"He existed before anything else, / and he holds all creation together" (Col. 1:17). God designed all creation to be dependent on Him. Humanity was designed to depend on God, and without such dependence death results. The essence of original sin was man's asserting his willfulness to be independent from God even though God provided everything necessary. "By his divine power, God has given us everything we need for living a godly life. We have received all of this by coming to know him, the one who called us to himself by means of his marvelous glory and excellence" (2 Peter 1:3).

The nature of our problem is that we work against God's established order and desire our independence from Him. Ultimately we want to depend on ourselves while being independent from God. We have adopted Satan's plan to be our own authority while seeking fulfillment in our physical life, quality of life, and even our eternal life. But still we are left incomplete. Our own desires block us from completeness in Christ.

God's design for life enables us on His terms. He requires brokenness, dependence, and obedience. Our eternal life begins at the point of salvation in a continuous relationship with God. As a result, our physical lives exist for God's purposes. God gives us everything we need for experiencing an abundant quality of life.

> For God in all his fullness
> was pleased to live in Christ,
> and through him God reconciled
> everything to himself.
> He made peace with everything in heaven and on earth
> by means of Christ's blood on the cross.

This includes you who were once far away from God. You were his enemies, separated from him by your evil thoughts and actions. Yet now he has reconciled you to himself through the death of Christ in his physical body. As a result, he has brought you into his own presence, and you are holy and blameless as you stand before him without a single fault.

—Col. 1:19–22

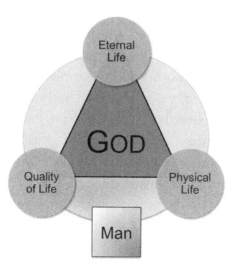

God's Design

I Want to Do It My Way

Man's desire is for God to empower life on our terms. From this perspective, all of life, including eternal life, is a pursuit of unending self-indulgence, unlimited pleasure, and unparalleled comfort. Our physical lives exist for our purposes; we believe we deserve everything we want. The perceived ultimate quality of life results from having the freedom to live life the way we think best.

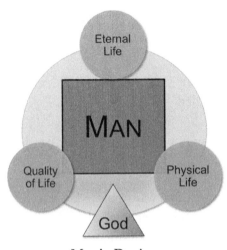

Man's Desire

Driven by the delusion that we can attain independence, we are convinced our fulfillment can only be addressed by our creative solutions. God may have a plan, but we don't see Him at work in our lives, so we will attempt to achieve satisfaction independently. We attach expectations for God to bring about our plans by employing all His power to accomplish our desires. Deceived, we come to the notion that God is perfectly OK with what we want. The delusion expands to accommodate the idea that our plans are equal to His will. From this perspective God exists for our gratification.

Our desire for independence clashes with the truth that only God is independent. We wrestle with futility as we strive to convince God that our plan should be His plan. With dashed hopes and thwarted expectations we grow resentful of God and stand in judgment of Him, doubting His love for us.

"What sorrow awaits those who argue with their Creator.
　　Does a clay pot argue with its maker?
Does the clay dispute with the one who shapes it, saying,
　　'Stop, you're doing it wrong!'
Does the pot exclaim,
　　'How clumsy can you be?'"

This is what the LORD says—
　　the Holy One of Israel and your Creator:
"Do you question what I do for my children?
　　Do you give me orders about the work of my hands?
I am the one who made the earth
　　and created people to live on it.
With my hands I stretched out the heavens.
　　All the stars are at my command."

　　　　　　　　　　　　　　　　　　　　　　　　—Isa. 45:9, 11–12

God responds that His will is *not* equal to our plans. Deafened by our delusions, we insist. Pretending to be sanctioned by the Lord, we amplify the deception moving us to a deeper level of darkness. "And they began to think up foolish ideas of what God was like. As a result, their minds became dark and confused. Claiming to be wise, they instead became utter fools" (Rom. 1:21–22). The battle intensifies between His will and our way.

"People ruin their lives by their own foolishness / and then are angry at the LORD" (Prov. 19:3).

I Can Do It My Way

In Galatians 5:22–23 God assures us, "The Holy Spirit produces this kind of fruit in our lives: love, joy, peace, patience, kindness, goodness, faithfulness, gentleness, and self-control" if we "follow the Spirit's leading in every part of our lives" (Gal. 5:25). The fruit of the Spirit encompasses the distinctiveness of God. No human plantation can create a vineyard such as His. God is the divine husbandman. He plants the vine and prunes it precisely to produce the fruit He wants. This fruit completes His portrait so the watching world can see a glimpse of Christ through our lives.

Over the next few chapters we will assess the fruit God wishes to produce through His Spirit. But in our desire for independence we attempt to counterfeit God's fruit with our own design. Desiring all He has for us, but not willing to give all we are to Him, we endeavor to circumvent His plan by producing our fruit of the flesh. Our miserable efforts culminate in disastrous results: emptiness, futility, turmoil, and frustration to name a few. Obtaining an education as a fruit inspector will prepare us to distinguish between the authentic fruit of the Spirit and the counterfeit fruit of the flesh.

Love > Self-Centeredness > Emptiness

Love is the fruit of the Holy Spirit that enables us to value others with the distinguishing characteristic of sacrificial giving for the best interest of another. God places within us the ability to value Him and others, producing the capability to give while expecting nothing in return. True love can be seen at the cross, where Christ willingly sacrificed everything to be in a relationship with us to fulfill the Father's purpose. Love promotes the work of God rather than the will of the individual. It is God's heart in action through us.

"Love is patient and kind. Love is not jealous or boastful or proud or rude. It does not demand its own way. It is not irritable, and it keeps no record of being wronged. It does not rejoice about injustice but rejoices whenever the truth wins out. Love never gives up, never loses faith, is always hopeful, and endures through every circumstance" (1 Cor. 13:4–7). God's fruit of love perfects our hearts with abilities that are alien to the human condition. We are not simply better versions of what we were; we are now something altogether different because of the Holy Spirit's work that moves us to Christlikeness.

Apart from God, the human heart has no capacity for love. Left to our own devices, we offer only a counterfeit version laden with self-interest as a means to secure our self-centered pleasures. We strive to attain value and worth through people, positions, and possessions, believing we can find fulfillment apart from Christ. This illicit love masquerades in forms that may look noble, but the chief concern is how something will impact self. The ideal of giving to another has been replaced by the idea of gaining for oneself.

By pursuing self-interest we contend with the toxic effects of frustration, hurt, fear, anger, and bitterness. The results of such are fatigue, resentment, depression, anxiety, the disintegration of relationships, and the ever-looming desire for more. These negative consequences perpetuate the unending cycle of spiritual and emotional depletion.

This pursuit of self-centeredness leads to emptiness. If you find yourself experiencing the symptom of emptiness, consider what self-centered means you are employing to counterfeit God's fruit of love.

We will evidence the fruit of love when we resign from the self-centeredness that culminates in emptiness and then allow the Holy Spirit to enable us to value others. "Dear friends, let us continue to love one another, for love comes from God. Anyone who loves is a child of God and knows God. But anyone who does not love does not know God, for God is love" (1 John 4:7–8).

Joy > Pleasure > Futility

Joy is the fruit of the Holy Spirit that reflects reliance on God. Jubilantly, a soul connected to Jesus gives tribute to God's redemptive work. When the conflicts of the heart have been resolved, joy is the result. Such a condition is simply the outward testimony that all is well within.

Joy is the expression of the trusting heart experiencing God—His power to live, His freedom from bondage, His promise of eternal fellowship. The transforming hand of God liberates a life from the prison of oppression when we yield to His design, resulting in joy.

People seem content to counterfeit joy with pleasure. The shackles of the sensual amusements of the world, the flesh, and the devil draw us through the lust of our hearts and the vanity of our lives and bind us in strongholds.

> Do not love this world nor the things it offers you, for when you love the world, you do not have the love of the Father in you. For the world offers only a craving for physical pleasure, a craving for everything we see, and pride in our achievements and possessions. These are not from the Father, but are from this world. And this world is fading away, along with everything that people crave. But anyone who does what pleases God will live forever.
>
> —1 John 2:15–17

Pleasure, however, does not have to be blatantly sinful. Yet all pleasure becomes sinful when we seek to be complete in it. When Jesus is left out of our lives, the pain of insatiable desires results in depriving us of the hope of fulfillment—futility. If you find yourself experiencing the symptom of futility, consider what means of pleasure you are employing to counterfeit God's fruit of joy.

"I said to myself, 'Come now, let's try pleasure. Let's look for the 'good things' in life.' But I found that this, too, was meaningless" (Eccles. 2:1). God's solution to the meaninglessness is found in our connection to Jesus.

> Remain in me, and I will remain in you. For a branch cannot produce fruit if it is severed from the vine, and you cannot be fruitful unless you remain in me.
>
> Yes, I am the vine; you are the branches. Those who remain in me, and I in them, will produce much fruit. For apart from me you can do nothing. Anyone who does not remain in me is thrown away like a useless branch and withers. Such branches are gathered into a pile to be burned. But if you remain in me and my words remain in you, you may ask for anything you want, and it will be granted! When you produce much fruit, you are my true disciples. This brings great glory to my Father.
>
> I have loved you even as the Father has loved me. Remain in my love. When you obey my commandments, you remain in my love, just as I obey my Father's commandments and remain in his love. I have told you these things so that you will be filled with my joy. Yes, your joy will overflow!
>
> —John 15:4–11

We will evidence the fruit of joy when we give up our futile pursuit of pleasure and choose reliance on God. "I pray that God, the source of hope, will fill you completely with joy and peace because you trust in him. Then you will overflow with confident hope through the power of the Holy Spirit" (Rom. 15:13).

Peace > Comfort > Turmoil

Peace is the fruit of the Holy Spirit that supplies security in Christ, who provides all that is needed for life and godliness. It is the evidence of one who is dependent on Christ to provide the ability to cope with the problems, pain, and perplexities of living. In the midst of conflict we can experience the absence of fear, dread, and impending doom as we rest in the presence of His safety, tranquility, and contentment. A continuous relationship with Jesus Christ overflows with peace that comes from entrusting every struggle to Him. There is strength in knowing that while all around us is in flux and failure, Jesus provides a spiritual stability beyond the normal boundaries of this existence. We experience peace in the presence of finding Christ relevant to our situation even when we cannot be in control.

Peace resides when the soul has been brought to balance by the work of Christ calming the turmoil of the heart. It is achieved by the release of self to the care of a trusted Savior, who in turn assures the individual of a promise of safekeeping that moves one to believe all is well.

"You will keep in perfect peace / all who trust in you, / all whose thoughts are fixed on you! / Trust in the LORD always, / for the LORD GOD is the eternal Rock" (Isa. 26:3–4).

Humanity desires a Christ-less comfort. Submission is too demanding and taxing and infringes on our sense of control. We choose rather to be at ease by creating an environment where the circumstances and situations favor us. Our relational connections to people, positions, and possessions serve to vanquish stress and strain. The pursuit of comfort most assuredly leads to all we have sought to avoid, and results in turmoil. While attempting to evade the pain of life, our quest for comfort brings the consequences of sin and illicit dependencies. Apart from God's empowerment, we settle for the feeble counterfeits of God substitutes. If you find yourself experiencing the symptom of turmoil, consider what means of comfort you are employing to counterfeit God's fruit of peace.

> This is what the LORD says—
> your Redeemer, the Holy One of Israel:
> "I am the LORD your God,
> who teaches you what is good for you
> and leads you along the paths you should follow.
> Oh, that you had listened to my commands!
> Then you would have had peace flowing like a gentle river
> and righteousness rolling over you like waves in the sea."
>
> —Isa. 48:17–18

We will evidence the fruit of peace when we cease our pursuit of comfort with its resulting turmoil and find our security through Christ instead. "Don't worry about anything; instead, pray about everything. Tell God what you need, and thank him for all he has done. Then you will experience God's peace, which exceeds anything we can understand. His peace will guard your hearts and minds as you live in Christ Jesus" (Phil. 4:6–7).

Patience > Control > Frustration

Patience is the fruit of the Holy Spirit that enables us to persevere under pressure. Patience maintains the virtues of love, joy, and peace when faced with the pressures of wrong, mistreatment, or taxation. When pressed, patience does not retaliate but rather addresses the underlying motivations of the soul. By His fruit of patience, the Holy Spirit moves us to look to Jesus for strength, giving the ability to forbear in circumstances that would otherwise deplete our resolve.

"Since God chose you to be the holy people he loves, you must clothe yourselves with tenderhearted mercy, kindness, humility, gentleness, and patience. Make allowance for each other's faults, and forgive anyone who offends you. Remember, the Lord forgave you, so you must forgive others" (Col. 3:12–13). The clothes we are to put on are tailor-made to fit our lives by the Spirit. Dressed in His power we are divinely enabled to accomplish the task He asks us to undertake. We cannot create our own style of patience; instead we are to put on His personally designed and custom-fitted attire. The royal garments of the King identify our position of servitude apart from personal ambition. We exhibit patience because He empowers us to do so, not because we have created it ourselves for our purpose.

When we attempt to counterfeit the Holy Spirit's line of designer clothing, our wardrobe quickly fills with costumes of control. With masks of all shapes and sizes we create the illusion that we are in control and are capable of controlling all that is around us. But inevitably life is a process of losing control. Even though our patience is so often taxed, and love, joy, and peace seem unattainable, we still choose to strategically control all aspects of our lives. We believe we can have patience when our expectations are being met. Therefore, the desire of the controlling heart is to guarantee a favorable outcome, maintaining self-interest, pleasure, and comfort through manipulation and exploitation of people, positions, and possessions.

Control must not be stereotyped as mean, hateful, angry, or limited to an aspect of gender, age, or population group. Control may be a little old grandmother who is terrified of one of her grandchildren getting hurt, so she seeks to use guilt, shame, and fear to limit their activities. Control may be an abusive husband who threatens to harm the wife if she tells anyone about the abuse. Control may be a rebellious teenager who climbs out the window at night to rendezvous with his choice of defiant activities. Control may be seen in homes, businesses, or even pulpits. If we are not living by the power of God, we are most certainly seeking to supply our own control.

Even though we try to control what we are incapable of controlling, we continue striving only to end in frustration. When we can't get what we want and want more than we have, the dissatisfaction motivates temper tantrums. After all, "I deserve what I want"; "I should be able to have what I want"; "You should give me what I want." Our self-centered world will inevitably come crashing down. Solomon admonished, "Patience of spirit is better than haughtiness of spirit" (Eccles. 7:8 NASB). Therefore, Paul advised, "Always be humble and gentle. Be patient with each other, making allowance for each other's faults because of your love. Make every effort to keep yourselves united in the Spirit, binding yourselves together with peace" (Eph. 4:2–3). The ability to accomplish this mission only comes through patience supplied by the fruit of the Spirit when we let go of our control and its resulting frustration. If you find yourself experiencing the symptom of frustration, consider what means of control you are employing to counterfeit God's fruit of patience.

Too often our dishonesty is apparent when we pretend we are exhibiting the fruit of the Spirit, when in actuality we are only displaying the counterfeit fruit of the flesh. When the culmination of the counterfeits becomes evident in our lives, our deception is unmasked. We create our own version of genuineness and attempt to convince those around us that we are virtuous. Without recognizing God's absolute truth, we elevate our personal perspective as truth that should be upheld. By espousing statements such as "I honestly believe you should …" we promote our beliefs above God's truth and deceive others. After all, we say, "I am being honest." Although we may assert we are being honest, we pervert the virtue of honesty to be equivalent to God's truth. Our so-called honesty is really a cover for being dishonest with God. We elevate our perception above God's truth. Believing our own deception, we prevent movement toward God. Psalm 119:29 acknowledges that we deceive ourselves. "Keep me from lying to myself; / give me the privilege of knowing your instructions." As we understand God's instructions more completely, we can destroy the power of the lies that keep us from desperately depending on God for our sufficiency. Free from the culminations of the counterfeits, we can experience the abundance of His authentic fruit.

We must realize that it is our attempts to be independent from God that are destroying our lives. God designed humanity to live in a relationship dependent on Him, but our desire is for God to empower life on our terms. God offers love, joy, peace, and patience, but we counterfeit His fruit by being self-centered, pleasure oriented, comfort seeking, and controlling. Our meager efforts culminate with emptiness, futility, turmoil, and frustration. We cannot have optimal fulfillment apart from what we were created to be: complete in Christ.

Insight Journal

Before you begin asking yourself these questions, ask God to show you what He wants you to see, and commit to striving to hear His Spirit speaking to you. You may be surprised to notice that as you allow God's heart to speak to yours, the lists will become longer and longer!

1. What keeps me from connecting to God?
2. What self-centered means have I employed to find love? What were the results?
3. When have I sought pleasure instead of relying on the Spirit's fruit of joy? What were the results?
4. What methods did I employ to find comfort when needing peace? What were the results?
5. What have I been trying to control? What were the results?

Psalms Prayer Pattern

I give you thanks, O Lord, with all my heart;
  I will sing your praises before the gods.
I bow before your holy Temple as I worship.
  I praise your name for your unfailing love and faithfulness;
for your promises are backed
  by all the honor of your name.
As soon as I pray, you answer me;
  you encourage me by giving me strength.

Every king in all the earth will thank you, Lord,
  for all of them will hear your words.
Yes, they will sing about the Lord's ways,
  for the glory of the Lord is very great.
Though the Lord is great, he cares for the humble,
  but he keeps his distance from the proud.

Though I am surrounded by troubles,
  you will protect me from the anger of my enemies.
You reach out your hand,
  and the power of your right hand saves me.
The Lord will work out his plans for my life—
  for your faithful love, O Lord, endures forever.
  Don't abandon me, for you made me.

—Ps. 138

CHAPTER 3

My Way Isn't Working

MAMA PAID A friendly visit to her hairstylist, and little Johnny Kirk discovered an inspiring plastic astronaut buried in the sand outside under an oak tree. Knowing the evil desires of my heart, Mama admonished me to not take the astronaut from its space. But from my point of view the astronaut had a mission to complete: he must explore the deep recesses of my pocket. When confronted by my mother, I continued in my innovative solutions and lied to cover my expedition. I saw the astronaut as a satisfaction of my aspiration to escape the gravitational pull of boredom and be a part of the space race. Creativity ignited as I contrived further explanations to cover my transgression, but ultimately the truth was exposed and I had to face the consequences of my ill-fated mission. Once again I was grounded.

It Has to Be My Way

Our efforts to control our lives produce undesirable results. But still we attempt to counterfeit God's design for our lives through our own efforts. With tenacity we persist in demanding that our way must work. And so we continue to counterfeit the fruit of the Holy Spirit. Deceived, we believe the fruit of the Spirit is merely the best side of humanity. If we try hard enough we can manufacture this fruit consistently in our lives. But living a life that is desperately dependent on Christ necessitates yielding to His Spirit's movement as we cease endeavoring to produce our own fruit. We are incapable of producing His fruit on our own vines; we can only produce His fruit as we are grafted into His vine.

Kindness > Manipulation > Anger

Kindness is the fruit of the Holy Spirit that enables us to show God's love. Since love is distinguished by how it treats others, then kindness is the essence of that treatment. When the fruit of the Spirit evidences kindness, it ministers sacrificially to the needs of others for no higher reason than to benefit another for God's glory. It is seeking another's best interest, not about getting what we want. Sacrificial giving is impossible to manufacture. It can only come as a fruit of God's Spirit in our lives. To surrender to the best interest of another moves in opposition to the very nature of our fleshly desire to promote and preserve self. Although we may appear altruistic, too often our actions are for a personal secondary gain.

Kindness is the means through which God transmits His love and goodwill to those in need. As we, by the power of the Holy Spirit, share kindness to others, we are in essence giving them the very nature of God's love. The vital riches of God flow through kindness as it touches the needs of the heart.

> But God is so rich in mercy, and he loved us so much, that even though we were dead because of our sins, he gave us life when he raised Christ from the dead. (It is only by God's grace that you have been saved!) For he raised us from the dead along with Christ and seated us with him in the heavenly realms because we are united with Christ Jesus. So God can point to us in all future ages as examples of the incredible wealth of his grace and kindness toward us, as shown in all he has done for us who are united with Christ Jesus.
>
> —Eph. 2:4–7

As a counterfeit, manipulation is the process of managing people, posturing into a position, and utilizing possessions as a means of achieving control. The objective of manipulation is to bring life resources (people, positions, possessions) under our domain of influence to promote our personal agenda, leading to what we believe will make us complete. Webster's defines *manipulate* as "to manage or utilize skillfully; to control or play upon by artful, unfair, or insidious means especially to one's own advantage."[1] Although manipulation is negative in intent, it may not always appear harmful.

We constantly swing between feeling in and out of control, drained by the stressors of manipulative living. Only for short intervals of time do we feel secure with the control fostered. Repeatedly we find ourselves hurt as a result of our attempts to manipulate others by producing kindness from our own resources. A downward spiral of anger, resentment, bitterness, and hate is produced because we did not receive the anticipated response as we look to others for our love, significance, and security. We desire affirmation for our efforts that have depleted our resources. Anger rises up within us in response to our thwarted efforts and is the indication that our expectations have not been met. Believing ourselves to have been devalued, we are left with hurt feelings. We fear we will never be satisfied and view the delinquent response to our manipulative efforts as depriving us of what is rightfully ours. We feel angry.

If we truly give from the overflow of kindness the Holy Spirit produces in our lives, the abundant supply would never run dry. Furthermore, because we are enjoying the Spirit's fruit, we no longer need to look to others for our love, significance, and security. We are complete in Christ. We can be free from the bondage of requiring constant affirmation to feel good about ourselves. If you find yourself experiencing the symptom of anger, consider what means of manipulation you may be employing to counterfeit God's fruit of kindness.

So how do we evidence God's kindness that the Holy Spirit instills in our lives? To show God's love we must give up our manipulation that results in anger. Colossians 3:12 reminds us again that we are to put on the garments His love has graciously supplied to us so we may share with others: "Since God chose you to be the holy people he loves, you must clothe yourselves with tenderhearted mercy, kindness, humility, gentleness, and patience."

Goodness > Exploitation > Inadequacy

Goodness is the fruit of the Holy Spirit that enables us to exemplify God's moral nature. When the Holy Spirit is resident in our lives, His qualities transform us into God's image, enabling us to treat others with holiness. That is goodness. It can only reflect what is godly. It bears no ill will and concerns itself only with the mind and mission of God to humanity.

Identifying Jesus as a good man, the rich young ruler was met with the following retort: "'Why do you call me good?' Jesus asked him. 'Only God is truly good'" (Luke 18:19). Because only God is good, only His Spirit can produce goodness in our lives. Goodness is a trademark of a life-exhibiting the character of Christ. Apart from a relationship with Him, goodness cannot be concocted.

The fruit of the flesh equates goodness with being nice. Unaided by God's Spirit we calculate how to behave in the most socially acceptable way to subtly access and use life resources to meet perceived needs. Like a wolf in sheep's clothing, exploitation conceals itself in the disguise of being nice. Exploitation thinks in terms of how the world benefits self. People, positions, and possessions are evaluated based on their utility for personal gain. Goodness operates without sinful intent, not violating others' God-given rights, with no hidden agendas, and springs from a relationship of purity. Exploitation concerns itself with the mind and mission of self to accomplish the four goals of the flesh.

- Promote the best interest of self
- Procure the greatest pleasure for self
- Promise the most comfort for self
- Produce the maximum control over self

The ultimate conclusion of attempting to accomplish these goals is the culmination of inadequacy. A sense of insufficiency seizes control when failure to achieve satisfaction highlights our weakness. The reality of this inadequacy mocks us with the folly of our way. We are inadequate in the role of God. We have no power to produce change within ourselves apart from the enabling of the Holy Spirit. Only through God can we exemplify goodness; otherwise we settle for merely being socially appropriate. If you find yourself experiencing the symptom of inadequacy, consider what means of exploitation you are employing to counterfeit God's fruit of goodness.

We will evidence the fruit of goodness when we forgo exploitation with its resulting inadequacy in order to exemplify Christ in all that we do. "Don't be selfish; don't try to impress others. Be humble, thinking of others as better than yourselves. Don't look out only for your own interests, but take an interest in others, too" (Phil. 2:3–4).

Faithfulness > Pretense > Anxiety

Magnificently, Christ sent the Holy Spirit to fill our lives with faith. Faithfulness is the fruit that enables us to trust Christ and rely continuously upon His truth. This fruit of faithfulness is not about our being worthy of trust, but recognizing God as being worthy of trust, which leads to a constant reliance on Him.

The faith given by the Spirit is intricately involved in connecting to God. It is essential to pleasing God and possessing His power. Through this divine fruit we can accomplish His purposes. Here again we see the reciprocal relationship of divine enablement leading to personal empowerment: "I can do all things through Him who strengthens me" (Phil. 4:13 NASB).

In our human declaration of independence, we confidently communicate we are full of faith. But the faith we possess is faith in ourselves instead of faith in Christ. Perhaps we attempt to convey we enjoy a significant relationship with Christ, but no impact is evident. "People may be right in their own eyes, / but the LORD examines their heart" (Prov. 21:2). Without a connection to truth that is facilitated by the Holy Spirit and the Word of God, we cannot even be aware of our pretense. "For the word of God is alive and powerful. It is sharper than the sharpest two-edged sword, cutting between soul and spirit, between joint and marrow. It exposes our innermost thoughts and desires" (Heb. 4:12). God wills for us to know the truth and He is constantly revealing truth. But when we demand our independence, we persist in the lies and perpetrate the pretense.

Too often we choose to counterfeit faith when we pretend we can handle everything. A crisis quickly exposes the pretense when anxiety invades. In the midst of anxiety we give mental energy to the resolving of our own problems as opposed to trusting God to resolve our problems. Our feeble attempts are lacking without genuine trust in Christ. Trust either waits on God to provide direction or it acts on what God has already instructed. If you find yourself experiencing the symptom of anxiety, consider what means of pretense you may be employing to counterfeit God's fruit of faithfulness.

"You should know this, Timothy, that in the last days there will be very difficult times....They will act religious, but they will reject the power that could make them godly" (2 Tim. 3:1, 5).

We will evidence the fruit of faithfulness when we lay aside our pretense and its resulting anxiety in exchange for trusting Christ. "And it is impossible to please God without faith. Anyone who wants to come to him must believe that God exists and that he rewards those who sincerely seek him" (Heb. 11:6).

Gentleness > Selfish Ambition > Alienation

Gentleness is the fruit of the Holy Spirit that enables us to reflect God's grace to the world. Grace is God's power to live that enables us to fulfill His will and be complete.

1 Cor 10:12, 13

12:11

The transforming presence of Christ establishes the order of our souls so we can convey God's grace through gentleness. As God's Spirit produces gentleness in our lives, He establishes our attitude, fashions our approach, and directs our actions with others. When we are blessed with the fruit of gentleness, His abundant supply must overflow into the lives of others. With humble selflessness we are compelled to transmit His power to live. We cannot be content with merely possessing the attitude of gentleness, but as representatives of God to others, we must display His fruit through our actions. "Who among you is wise and understanding? Let him show by his good behavior his deeds in the gentleness of wisdom" (James 3:13 NASB).

Without God's grace, selfish ambition asserts, "I must be served"; "My way must be followed"; and "I am right." Having control over life's resources is seen as the priority and must be the object of life's pursuit. Selfish ambition is not concerned with the welfare of others but with the power we have over our domain. It is through this perception of strength that we derive our sense of self-sufficiency. With continuous resolve we persist in our selfish ambition.

Our exhausted supply of resources leaves us alienated. Loneliness invades as our thwarted efforts become evident. The emptiness of our hearts tempts us to continue the vicious cycle of seeking God-substitutes to fill the void. With continued resolve we contrive another plan of employing people, positions, and possessions for our power to live. Eventually the futility of the endeavor becomes evident through social rejection, compromised health, and a lack of personal energy to pursue the pathological dream. Alienated souls now stand stranded beside the road they thought would take them to the place of completion. "See, they are all foolish, worthless things. / All your idols are as empty as the wind" (Isa. 41:29). If you find yourself experiencing the symptom of alienation, consider what means of selfish ambition you are employing to counterfeit God's fruit of gentleness.

We can exemplify the fruit of gentleness when we relinquish our selfish ambition and its resulting alienation. Enabled by the Spirit, I can reflect God's grace. "Gently instruct those who oppose the truth. Perhaps God will change those people's hearts, and they will learn the truth" (2 Tim. 2:25).

My Behaviors Are My Solutions

In spite of our best efforts, our behaviors are only *our* inadequate solutions aimed at resolving the deeper problem. This deeper problem cannot be resolved by our own power no matter how diligent the endeavor. The implementation of our solutions drives our lives. We utilize all our energy and try to employ others to facilitate our remedy. But as we pursue various resolutions to this deeper problem, we only add more problems to our lives. It permeates all we do.

The deeper problem is best defined as the nature of sin that resides within all of us. This nature of sin is incorporated into the essence of who we are. All aspects of our being are infected, not just affected, by sin. This sin nature controls our desires and the behaviors we choose, and establishes our state of being. Because of the sin nature life is dominated by guilt, shame, fear, anger, loneliness, and a propensity to seek self-interest. "But there is another power within me that is at war with my mind. This power makes me a slave to the sin that is still within me" (Rom. 7:23).

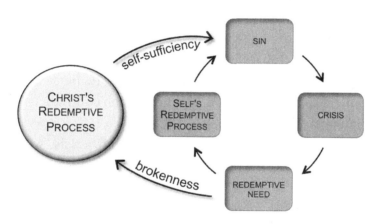

The Problem

The nature of our sin produces continual crisis. Our current line of solutions is not working to resolve the guilt, shame, and fear inherent to the sinfulness. Emptiness, low self-esteem, loneliness, and perfectionism are the manifestations of the symptoms festering in our souls. We want to say, "My boss is a jerk"; "My spouse is not meeting my needs"; "My kids aren't measuring up to my standards"; "My career is not satisfying"; but these things are not the real crisis. The real crisis is that our way isn't working to resolve the manifestations of sin. We are alienated from God. We are looking for new solutions. We are dissatisfied with others and ourselves. Therefore self-centeredness escalates the crisis. Self-centeredness is the embodiment of our sinfulness. The character of sin is exposed through the <u>promotion and preservation of self</u>. The unresolved issues of the nature of sin within us create the mounting pressures of life, stress, anxiety, depression, and all predicaments encountered. Our daily crisis results from the resident sin.

In an attempt to resolve our crisis produced by the nature of sin, we seek deliverance. God has designed us to live within a context of love, joy, and peace. We are not designed to live in a constant state of pressure, stress, and anxiety. But the nature of sin brings these traumatizing by-products along with the guilt, shame, and fear that are embedded in the sin nature. The craving for love, joy, and peace is a <u>residual part of the image of God lying dormant within our souls that is searching for redemption.</u> We cannot stay in our crisis. The need for restored control and resulting peace prompt the search. Motivated by crisis, people inevitably embrace their redemptive need. Invariably this promotes a redemptive process to meet the redemptive demand.

Although God desires His creation to seek Him for redemption, we continue to devise our own salvation strategies to dissipate the conflicts. Compelled by the redemptive need, all of humanity will either employ self's redemptive process, or choose participation in Christ's redemptive process. Self-effort naturally embraces the lie of the sin nature that states we can be complete apart from Christ. This perversion contradicts God's truth that we can only be complete in Christ.

Independent inclinations thrust individuals further into crisis, which perpetuates an unending cycle of futility. At best, self-effort can only temporarily affect the crisis of our lives; it can do nothing to address the deeper problem of sin. In fact, self-effort exacerbates the problem, actually increasing the intensity of the nature of sin's impact on us. Now we have, as a result of our best solutions, even more guilt, shame, and fear. We are even more alienated from God than before. We only sink deeper into the bondage of our sinfulness. Because of humanity's depravity, we are stuck in the unending, self-perpetuating cycle. Demoting God as the authority; promoting self as the authority; and exploiting people, positions, and possessions for personal empowerment characterize self's redemptive process.

We look for relief from the resources of the flesh. A life-altering effect may be employed by addiction, deviance, mental illness, or death. Addiction chooses God substitutes to control the crisis' impact on us, either by sedating or stimulating us to euphoria. Deviance breaks social norms to resolve the crisis by changing our life's condition to be more favorable to us, albeit at the expense of others. To avoid responsibility and accountability, one may retreat into mental illness in an effort to hide with a diagnosis as an excuse. The ultimate perverted option to negate the crisis is death. This may be evidenced by risk-taking behaviors, a death wish, homicide, or suicide.

The fallout from independently contrived solutions intensifies the symptoms of the sin nature, thereby provoking an even greater crisis. No matter what we do, we are still falling apart. We are still at the place of redemptive need. Only God can help us.

Christ's redemptive process can only be participated in through the power of Christ as He addresses the nature of sin by bringing us to brokenness. The willingness to give up our willfulness to Christ in exchange for His enabling us to submit to His will, removes our resistance to entering into Christ's redemptive process. Christ's redemptive process is characterized by dependence on Him as we see ourselves in desperate need of Him.

Because of Christ's satisfaction of the sin debt, He can redeem us from our sinful selves and all the crises we have created. He resolves the symptoms of the sin nature—guilt, shame, and fear—and reconciles us to fellowship with God, restoring love, joy, and peace. "He himself is the sacrifice that atones for our sins—and not only our sins but the sins of all the world" (1 John 2:2).

Unfortunately, we must still contend with the nature of sin resident within us. Self-sufficiency tempts us to reenter the futile cycle dominated by the nature of sin in our lives. But gratefully, at the point of salvation, we are blessed with a new set of options. No longer are we bound by the power of sin; we may now choose from His abundant resources and allow His divine enablement to personally empower us.

> By his divine power, God has given us everything we need for living a godly life. We have received all of this by coming to know him, the one who called us to himself by means of his marvelous glory and excellence. And because of his glory and excellence, he has given us great and precious promises. These are the promises that enable you to share his divine nature and escape the world's corruption caused by human desires.
>
> —2 Peter 1:3–4

I Want What I Want

The familiar story of Jonah illustrates the approaches employed to address the deeper problem of the nature of sin. God was seeking to save a people while salvaging a prophet.

Resistance and self-sufficiency jumped to the forefront as fear, evidenced by anger, gripped Jonah's heart at the thought that God would not judge the wicked Ninevites. Jonah's strategy to resolve the crisis was to ensure that God would destroy the people of Nineveh. Believing he could thwart God's plan by refusing to participate, Jonah asserted his willfulness to create his own redemptive process. Unwilling to trust God, Jonah allowed his bitterness to fester and employed his own creative solutions.

The command to obey God produced a crisis for Jonah, the messenger of God. The possibility of God being merciful and compassionate to Nineveh pressured him to the point of stress and anxiety. Advancing his way over God's will, Jonah attempted to resolve the crisis and restore control to himself, prompting Jonah to address his redemptive need with a plan to go in the opposite direction to get away from the Lord.

Prompted by the lie that he could actually live independently, Jonah boarded a ship, hoping to escape from the Lord. Temporary relief came as he slept in the hold of the ship. God disrupted Jonah's comfort with a storm prepared especially for him. Invested in ignoring God, Jonah also shut out the thrashing of the waves, the pitch and yaw of the ship, and the shifting of the cargo until the captain of the ship demanded Jonah seek his God for a redemptive plan. What irony!

But Jonah sought to resolve the crisis with another self-made plan involving a death wish: "Throw me into the sea" (Jonah 1:12). In the belly of the great fish God once again offered His redemptive plan. After three days and three nights Jonah was ready to follow God's truth and acknowledged, "My salvation comes from the LORD alone" (2:9). Submitting to God's plan, he allowed the power of God to resolve his fears and take over his will.

"Then the LORD spoke to Jonah a second time:…This time Jonah obeyed" (3:1, 3). When the people of Nineveh "put a stop to their evil ways" (3:10), Jonah's greatest fear came true. An additional crisis was produced, and depression followed. Jonah's submission to God's will did not include adopting God's heart. He had no desire to see the people saved who were steeped in perversion and debauchery. Self-sufficiency regained its foothold, and with another death wish Jonah pleaded, "Just kill me now, LORD! I'd rather be dead than alive if what I predicted will not happen" (4:3). Invested in his own plan, his depression intensified while he justified his mental illness. "The LORD replied, 'Is it right for you to be angry about this?'…'Yes,' Jonah retorted, 'even angry enough to die!'" (4:4, 9). The story ends with God in the process of salvaging

Jonah by showing him he has no ability to independently restore control to his life, because God's plan will prevail.

Despite our best efforts, our plans cannot measure up to God's design. Our feeble attempts to live independently from God result in disastrous consequences. Perversion propels us to further crisis, although God continues to assert His truth that we must be desperately dependent on Him in every area of our lives. Through Christ's redemptive process we have a new set of options that can overcome guilt, shame, and fear with an overflow of His love, joy, and peace if we are willing to be desperately dependent.

Insight Journal

Remember, in Galatians 5:22–23 God assures us, "The Holy Spirit produces this kind of fruit in our lives: love, joy, peace, patience, kindness, goodness, faithfulness, gentleness, and self-control" if we "follow the Spirit's leading in every part of our lives" (Gal. 5:25). This fruit completes His portrait in our lives so the watching world can see a glimpse of Christ. But in our desire for independence, we attempt to counterfeit God's fruit with our own design.

1. What do I need to let go of so the Holy Spirit's fruit can be evidenced in my life?

2. When would the following situations be ministry (seeking your best interest) versus manipulation (seeking my best interest)?
   a. Saying "I love you."
   b. "Come on over for dinner."
   c. "Let me introduce you to my friend."

3. Describe a situation in which you used exploitation instead of relying on the Spirit's fruit of goodness. How would this situation be described differently if you were relying on the Spirit's fruit of kindness?

4. Describe a situation in which you used pretense instead of relying on the Spirit's fruit of faithfulness. How would this situation be described differently if you were relying on the Spirit's fruit of faithfulness?

5. Describe a situation in which you used selfish ambition instead of relying on the Spirit's fruit of gentleness. How would this situation be described differently if you were relying on the Spirit's fruit of gentleness?

Psalms Prayer Pattern

Oh, what joy for those
    whose disobedience is forgiven,
    whose sin is put out of sight!
Yes, what joy for those
    whose record the Lord has cleared of guilt,
    whose lives are lived in complete honesty!
When I refused to confess my sin,
    my body wasted away,
    and I groaned all day long.
Day and night your hand of discipline was heavy on me.
    My strength evaporated like water in the summer heat. *Interlude*

Finally, I confessed all my sins to you
    and stopped trying to hide my guilt.
I said to myself, "I will confess my rebellion to the Lord."
    And you forgave me! All my guilt is gone. *Interlude*

Therefore, let all the godly pray to you while there is still time,
    that they may not drown in the floodwaters of judgment.
For you are my hiding place;
    you protect me from trouble.
    You surround me with songs of victory. *Interlude*

The Lord says, "I will guide you along the best pathway for your life.
    I will advise you and watch over you.
Do not be like a senseless horse or mule
    that needs a bit and bridle to keep it under control."

Many sorrows come to the wicked,
    but unfailing love surrounds those who trust the Lord.
So rejoice in the Lord and be glad, all you who obey him!
    Shout for joy, all you whose hearts are pure!

—Ps. 32

CHAPTER 4

All about Me

ANOTHER SCHOOL ASSIGNMENT required a variety of tasks to convey "All about Me." Poems, narratives, songs, raps, art projects, picture displays, family trees, and a myriad of other activities were employed to describe characteristics such as "What makes me happy"; "Where I live"; and "What I want to be when I grow up." What a challenge to communicate everything that makes me happy! Even in our earliest years, happiness is featured as the ultimate goal in life.

What Makes Me Happy

We want to be happy. God wants us to be happy. We want our spouses to be happy. We want our kids to be happy. We just want everyone to be happy. We especially want everyone to be happy with us. This is the American dream—we all deserve to be happy. But the American dream spawns the American nightmare. The pursuit of this dream leads to addiction, deviance, mental illness, and death, because it is ultimately based in self-centeredness.

Those who are dominated by the sinful nature think about sinful things, but those who are controlled by the Holy Spirit think about things that please the Spirit. So letting your sinful nature control your mind leads to death. But letting the Spirit control your mind leads to life and peace. For the sinful nature is always hostile to God. It never did obey God's laws, and it never will.

—Rom. 8:5–7

Let's examine the final descriptor of the fruit of the Spirit from Galatians 5 and see how it relates to our pursuit of happiness.

Self-Control > Self-Indulgence > Discouragement

The presence of God's Holy Spirit in our lives offers us the fruit of self-control. Self-control is the fruit that enables us to deny self. This is not the ability to control ourselves, but it is the freedom from being controlled by the desires of the flesh. Through divine enablement we are empowered to say no to our personal desires. Here, we have been granted the divine ability to fulfill the will of God by saying yes to the desires of the Spirit (Gal. 5:16–17, 24).

Yet self-indulgence, as counterfeiting self-control, emphasizes the putting off of personal restraint and giving in to the desires of fleshly longings. Only when the desire is certainly more painful than it is potentially pleasurable does one say no. The flesh will barely refuse gratification when certain pain is obvious and the destructive consequences are seen as immediate, undeniable, and depriving pleasure. Hence there must be a discernible level of self-indulgence found in self-restraint before the flesh is willing to concede. Otherwise, we opt to give in to whatever is pleasurable and self-fulfilling.

It is accurate to proclaim that the crown and glory of all the fruit of the flesh is self-indulgence. It is the expected reward for having labored in the vineyard of self-centeredness. Happiness is the illusive prize.

Our interest in indulgence is proportionate to our self-centeredness. The more we are concerned with self-promotion and self-preservation, the more we yearn to be indulged. We say, in essence, "Because I want to be promoted, I want you to promote me. Without your efforts on my behalf, I feel I am being deprived of what is necessary to make me happy. I expect you to promote and serve my interest."

The continuous pursuit of pleasure-producing indulgences culminates in discouragement. The eventual outcome of self-indulgence is discouragement because we want what we want, but our wants are never satisfied. Then we move to a new set of desires, believing these new choices will produce the ultimate fulfillment. This may even be labeled as a midlife crisis. Perhaps you did not have the family you wanted, the body shape and size you desired, the socioeconomic status you preferred, or your ideal job. Maybe you have been striving to make someone else happy, or you want him or her to make you happy. But you never settle in the place of contentment, and so you continue your search, only to end in despair and discouragement.

Discouragement embodies the loss of hope that we can promote and preserve self in a fashion that will produce the greatest fulfillment. Provoked by the inability to effect environmental changes to generate love, significance, and security, we continue with self-indulgence. Discouragement pervades over the fact that we have failed to create a platform powerful enough to make a difference in our lives that would sedate our emotional concerns or stimulate our ambitious yearnings.

Consider this example of a husband with three children who is unfaithful to his wife. He does not want to leave his wife, but he wants to have his girlfriend. He lies, deceives, and connives to keep one a secret and the other satisfied. It all comes to be exposed: "You may be sure that your sin will find you out" (Num. 32:23). The children come to hate their father. The father wants the kids to love him, he wants to continue with his wife, and he wants to keep his girlfriend. Instead, he loses everything he had and everything he hoped to gain.

"The LORD is our God, the LORD alone. And you must love the LORD your God with all your heart, all your soul, and all your strength" (Deut. 6:4–5).

Ultimately there is nothing that can impart contentment apart from Christ. We flit from bloom to bloom looking for the nectar of life, but only God is able to provide true satisfaction. The spiritual fruit of self-control is experienced through dependence on the Spirit of God so we do not have to depend on ourselves. His divine enablement leads to personal empowerment. If you find yourself experiencing the symptom of discouragement, consider what means of self-indulgence you are employing to counterfeit God's fruit of self-control.

As we submit to the Holy Spirit, we will see evidence of the Spirit's fruit of self-control in our lives when we renounce self-indulgence that gives way to discouragement. "Those who are dominated by the sinful nature think about sinful things, but those who are controlled by the Holy Spirit think about things that please the Spirit. So letting your sinful nature control your mind leads to death. But letting the Spirit control your mind leads to life and peace" (Rom. 8:5–6).

Where I Live

Erroneously we believe we must contrive the fruit of the Spirit by force of our human will. When we are told we must exhibit the fruit of the Spirit, we diligently work to manufacture the formula for accomplishing that task. When we recognize that we cannot produce His fruit through our own ability, we realize it is only as we experience Christ as relevant that His fruit comes alive within us with transforming power. It is by the process of divine intervention as we submit to His Spirit that we are enabled to be more than we are. Only as we depend on the Holy Spirit can we experience the fruit He has to offer. Then we can blossom with spiritual fruit. (See appendix A for complete Fruit Chart.)

Some will continue to hold on to self-effort while lamenting their inability to achieve His promised fruit. Propagating their self-contrived delusion, they assert that God is mistreating them and showing favoritism to others. They infer that either they are not good enough or God does not love them. This chant of perpetual defeat only serves to present a false image of virtue. In reality the individual does not want to let go of self-effort. The person is not willing to die to the flesh and live unto the Spirit. He or she says, "There must be some way to be spiritual my way. There must be a way I can access the riches of God through human means. Certainly God will allow me to govern my life while utilizing His power." We want the resource of grace apart from dependence on God. The problem of most spiritual struggles is not "I can't" but "I don't want to." In actuality, the lack of connectedness to Jesus is really the result of a decision to not die to self.

We are even tempted to look at the world around us and point to people we believe are successful. "So-and-so makes good choices and does just fine without God." But whose perspective really counts? How many times have we been convinced that a particular couple has the perfect marriage, only to hear they are getting a divorce? But even if the person under consideration who is apart from God believes, "I am just fine, thank you very much," God's Word clarifies the absolute truth.

At our best we cannot be more than what we are apart from Him. If we can't be other than what we are, then it would stand to reason that at most we could only be the best of what we are. The issue of concern now is "What am I?" "What do I really consist of?" If there is no good in us, then the best of what we are is devoid of goodness. If there is no love in us, then the best of what we are is devoid of love. If we are deceived, the best of what we are is living out our deception. If we are sinful, then the best of what we can do is to live out our sinfulness.

As the Scriptures say,

"No one is righteous—
    not even one.
No one is truly wise;
    no one is seeking God.
All have turned away;
    all have become useless.
No one does good,
    not a single one."
"Their talk is foul, like the stench from an open grave.
    Their tongues are filled with lies."
"Snake venom drips from their lips."
    "Their mouths are full of cursing and bitterness."
"They rush to commit murder.
    Destruction and misery always follow them.
They don't know where to find peace."
    "They have no fear of God at all."

—Rom. 3:10–18

This is the human being in our natural condition, unaided by the Spirit of God.

Even within Christianity we have made room for our own carnality. We want to follow God in a manner that seems interesting and stimulating to our flesh. Our walk becomes infected with selfish ambition and vain conceit, while we wear the garb of the righteous. Because we do not know how to connect to the Holy Spirit, we contrive our own version of His will: "It would make me happy to do what God wants, and I believe God wants me to …" As we learn to understand and obey His commands directly outlined in His Word, it becomes easier to listen and follow His still small voice when He specifically whispers to our hearts. But our quenching of the Holy Spirit is almost as frequent as His convicting of our sinfulness. Pursuing the flesh then becomes the mission of our faith. The issue is for self to be promoted and preserved while we pose as those who walk with God. "Outwardly you look like righteous people, but inwardly your hearts are filled with hypocrisy and lawlessness" (Matt. 23:28). "So we are lying if we say we have fellowship with God but go on living in spiritual darkness; we are not practicing the truth. But if we are living in the light, as God is in the light, then we have fellowship with each other, and the blood of Jesus, his Son, cleanses us from all sin" (1 John 1:6–7).

The condition of "living in spiritual darkness" can be exemplified in statements such as "I love the Lord"; "I'm trusting Him"; "I'm willing to do whatever He wants me to do." These assertions are proven to be false in our lives when they infringe on what we want. Then we are quick to abandon our professed loyalties to God in pursuit of what will make us comfortable. We deviate from His path to follow our own agenda.

The reality is that we live for the purpose of fulfilling our agenda of achieving happiness. It is difficult for us to admit we have an agenda; we want to deny selfish ambition in our decision-making processes. But the Bible reveals the hidden truth.

> "The human heart is the most deceitful of all things,
>   and desperately wicked.
>   Who really knows how bad it is?
> But I, the LORD, search all hearts
>   and examine secret motives.
> I give all people their due rewards,
>   according to what their actions deserve."
>
> —Jer. 17:9–10

We want to be able to disguise our self-centeredness. Who wants to be labeled as selfish? But we are incapable of accurately evaluating ourselves. God must reveal our condition to us as we draw so close to Him that His light can make all things clear. We must desire to see the truth of who we really are and who God really is. We can never come to God without truth, because truth brings us to God.

When the truth is revealed, we may be surprised to find these disturbing realities:

- My agenda is whatever will make me happy.
- I do not want to come to God to complete His agenda.
- I want to come to God so He can empower my agenda.
- Instead of serving God, I want God to serve me.
- I want to be self-centered, and I want God to approve.
- I want God to help me be more independent, more self-sufficient.
- I want God to empower me to not need Him.

- I do not just want to be independent; I want to be happy.
- I want all God's benefits in addition to all my desires.

Living for the purpose of fulfilling our own agenda is the result of seeing ourselves as independent. We believe we are capable of handling our own lives. We believe we don't need anyone guiding our lives. We don't need God except for His assistance in fulfilling our will. We see God and others as relevant only as they cooperate with what we want. When God and others do not fulfill our expectations, we develop anger and resentment. We are not happy because God has not measured up to our expectations, nor have others fulfilled our expectations. God cannot be trusted. God has been dishonest. Instead of condemning self, we condemn God. Either way, we move toward dependency on ourselves instead of God.

Distortions result in our belief system when we allow ourselves to become judgmental. We say, "If God loved me, God would do what I want Him to do. If you loved me, you would do what I want you to do." Toxic hurt and disappointment flow from the notion that if God valued us He would have met our expectations. Because He didn't meet our expectations, He doesn't value us. If God doesn't value us, He doesn't care. Therefore, we cannot depend on Him, and we must do it all ourselves and become our own god. What a terrible downward cycle is produced!

Having now ascended to the throne of our own lives, we seek to meet our perceived needs by exploiting others. Not only do we become our own god, but we also position ourselves as god in the lives of others. We convey the philosophy, "I know what is your best interest. Do it my way and happiness will be achieved." We place ourselves in the role of god and assert that if an individual follows our prescriptions that person will be blessed. What a contradiction to God's design.

"Oh, the joys of those who trust the Lord" (Ps. 40:4).

Since we operate on the idea that everything around us is designed for our own fulfillment, we think another's happiness will be achieved when that person fulfills our agenda. We are not exploiting the person, just redefining our role as his or her savior. We say, essentially, "If you do it my way, your needs will be met. You will be happy as you make me happy."

The reality of our hidden agenda reveals that whenever possible we're going to work to satisfy our own will. Control is our way of life, our passion, what gets us out of bed in the morning.

What I Want to Be When I Grow Up

Jubilantly, biblical truth redefines happiness. Happiness, by God's standard, is a state of well-being that is independent of all that is of this earth and dependent on all that is divine. It is the outcome of connecting to God in a manner that changes the innermost parts of our souls, giving rise to the fruit of His spirit. The protective barrier of truth that wards off anything that would attack our courage maintains this happiness.

> Look here, you who say, "Today or tomorrow we are going to a certain town and will stay there a year. We will do business there and make a profit." How do you know what your life will be like tomorrow? Your life is like the morning fog—it's here a little while, then it's gone. What you ought to say is, "If the Lord wants us to, we will live and do this or that." Otherwise you are boasting about your own plans, and all such boasting is evil. Remember, it is sin to know what you ought to do and then not do it.
>
> —James 4:13–17

The happiness spoken of in the Bible exists apart from worldly endeavors. Contrary to human wisdom, we do not need the right people, the right positions, or the right possessions to be happy. "Don't put your confidence in powerful people; / there is no help for you there" (Ps. 146:3). "Then he said, 'Beware! Guard against every kind of greed. Life is not measured by how much you own'" (Luke 12:15).

In fact, the pursuit of happiness through the avenues of life resources is sure to lead to the loss of happiness and will establish the foundation for all varieties of addiction. To independently seek happiness constitutes the surest way to become lost amid the maze of life's self-centered options.

> Then he told them a story: "A rich man had a fertile farm that produced fine crops. He said to himself, 'What should I do? I don't have room for all my crops.' Then he said, 'I know! I'll tear down my barns and build bigger ones. Then I'll have room enough to store all my wheat and other goods. And I'll sit back and say to myself, "My friend, you have enough stored away for years to come. Now take it easy! Eat, drink, and be merry!"'
>
> "But God said to him, 'You fool! You will die this very night. Then who will get everything you worked for?'
>
> "Yes, a person is a fool to store up earthly wealth but not have a rich relationship with God."
>
> —Luke 12:16–21

Solomon asserts that we are to pursue truth, not happiness. Why? People are incapable of discerning what is in their best interest. Proverbs cites the following reasons:

(1) We are given to self-justification.
   "All a man's ways seem right to him" (21:2 NIV).
(2) We are not capable of being satisfied.
   "Just as Death and Destruction are never satisfied, / so human desire is never satisfied" (27:20).
(3) We are given to a delusion of happiness.
   "They are pure in their own eyes, / but they are filthy and unwashed" (30:12).
(4) We allow pride to prevail.
   "Pride goes before destruction, / and haughtiness before a fall" (16:18).

So what is the solution? "Get the truth and never sell it; / also get wisdom, discipline, and good judgment" (23:23). "Don't be impressed with your own wisdom. / Instead, fear the LORD and turn away from evil" (3:7).

The issue of happiness is introduced in "The Blessed Man" passages of Scripture. (See appendix B for a listing of these passages.) Happiness, however, does not generally appear as the subject of these passages, but rather the adjective describing the state of those who are rightly connected to God. The truly blessed man, or the happy person, should not seek to enjoy happiness as a primary pursuit, but should rather seek to connect with God. Happiness occurs as the by-product of connecting to God. It is self-indulgence that motivates us to connect to God for the attainment of happiness. Often Christianity is billed as the elixir of life to ensure happiness. This misses the mark of Christianity's real purpose—to experience God through the blood of Jesus Christ and to glorify Him. Encountering God produces happiness. To avoid the "What's in it for me?" syndrome, happiness must not be held up as the ultimate virtue for the Christian.

One may ask, "Then why would a person come to Jesus if not to gain happiness?" The Bible asserts that we were drawn to God not by the potential of happiness but by the aura of His glory and virtue (2 Peter 1:4). Upon being enlightened by God, His image within us attracts us to Himself. By Him we were created, through Him we consist, for Him we exist. Thus for Him we yearn. Reconciliation to God is the core need of the soul; therefore, connection to Christ becomes our deepest desire. We come to God because it is within His design that we need someone who is greater than ourselves to direct our lives. Our souls long for God and the fellowship He offers through the forgiveness of sins and the communion of His Spirit. If I merely come to Christ to feel good, believing I can escape hell, this fire insurance will not keep my house from burning down or my soul from eternal separation from God.

Happiness is derived when we encounter God and connect with Him spiritually. Jesus spoke of the spiritual encounter with His Father to the Samaritan woman. "But the time is coming—indeed it's here now—when true worshipers will worship the Father in spirit and in truth. The Father is looking for those who will worship Him that way. For God is Spirit, so those who worship Him must worship in spirit and in truth" (John 4:23–24).

The spirit Jesus spoke of was the spirit of our own souls where God desires to encounter us. The human soul is the temple of the spirit where we meet with God to commune with Him personally. Each one of us possesses our own personal temple; our own personal rooms where we may, at any time, sit and encounter God in meaningful fellowship—heart to heart. Judging from the Samaritan woman's response to meeting Jesus spiritually, we must attest to the fact that such an encounter is life changing.

> The woman said, "I know the Messiah is coming—the one who is called Christ. When he comes, he will explain everything to us." Then Jesus told her, "I AM the Messiah!"... The woman left her water jar beside the well and ran back to the village, telling everyone, "Come and see a man who told me everything I ever did! Could he possibly be the Messiah?"
>
> —John 4:25–29

Spirituality enabled this woman to see beyond Jesus' humanity into His deity. Perhaps the reason it is so hard to experience Jesus as real and relevant is because we are not seeking Him in spirit and truth.

Many attempt to substitute another process for this dynamic one. They would rather connect to happiness through sensuality, sexuality, emotionality, and all varieties of counterfeits. They would rather bypass spirituality, except when it may be used to gain false assurance, and seek happiness through compulsive behaviors that either stimulate or sedate.

Unless our lives are God-centered, we are self-centered. We place ourselves in the position of God and try to fulfill His role in the lives of the people around us. In our delusion, we strive to satisfy our desires while exploiting life resources.

In order to be desperately dependent on God we must confront the deception—our independence is leading us away from Him. It is essential to experience Him as relevant in every area of our lives while we apply truth concerning Jesus to the challenges of our lives. When we see Christ as relevant in our lives, we desire Him. As we desire Him, we draw into a closer love relationship with Him. Repentance is required to turn from our self-indulgence to finding our satisfaction in Christ alone. He is all we need.

The ultimate reality is that God did not design happiness as our life goal. God designed us to be in an intimate relationship with Him. Therefore, all of our life endeavors should be fostering our connection to Him as we conform to His image.

Insight Journal

1. This is how I would describe me:
2. I remember a time in my life when I tried to pursue my own desires but ended up with discouragement, even though I attained my goal. (Write the story.)
3. What is my personal agenda for my life? (You may want to review the list of "disturbing realities" given in this chapter.)
4. What am I pursuing to make me happy?
5. When do I feel most connected to God? What keeps me from residing at that place?

Psalms Prayer Pattern

Bend down, O Lord, and hear my prayer;
>   answer me, for I need your help.
Protect me, for I am devoted to you.
>   Save me, for I serve you and trust you.
>   You are my God.
Be merciful to me, O Lord,
>   for I am calling on you constantly.
Give me happiness, O Lord,
>   for I give myself to you.
O Lord, you are so good, so ready to forgive,
>   so full of unfailing love for all who ask for your help.
Listen closely to my prayer, O Lord;
>   hear my urgent cry.
I will call to you whenever I'm in trouble,
>   and you will answer me.

No pagan god is like you, O Lord.
>   None can do what you do!
All the nations you made
>   will come and bow before you, Lord;
>   they will praise your holy name.
For you are great and perform wonderful deeds.
>   You alone are God.

Teach me your ways, O Lord,
>   that I may live according to your truth!
Grant me purity of heart,
>   so that I may honor you.
With all my heart I will praise you, O Lord my God.
>   I will give glory to your name forever,
for your love for me is very great.
>   You have rescued me from the depths of death.

O God, insolent people rise up against me;
    a violent gang is trying to kill me.
    You mean nothing to them.
But you, O Lord,
    are a God of compassion and mercy,
slow to get angry
    and filled with unfailing love and faithfulness.
Look down and have mercy on me.
    Give your strength to your servant;
    save me, the son of your servant.
Send me a sign of your favor.
    Then those who hate me will be put to shame,
    for you, O Lord, help and comfort me.

—Ps. 86

CHAPTER 5

My Portrait of God

EVEN BEFORE THE world began there was a debate about how God should operate. Angelic beings and humans alike have contrived multiple ideas about God and how He should conduct the affairs of the universe. Similarly, we erroneously contrive our own portrait of God based on how we believe He should rule the world. Convinced that we have a better idea, we envision life from our skewed perspective.

But God shows his anger from heaven against all sinful, wicked people who suppress the truth by their wickedness. They know the truth about God because he has made it obvious to them. For ever since the world was created, people have seen the earth and sky. Through everything God made, they can clearly see his invisible qualities—his eternal power and divine nature. So they have no excuse for not knowing God.

Yes, they knew God, but they wouldn't worship him as God or even give him thanks. And they began to think up foolish ideas of what God was like. As a result, their minds became dark and confused. Claiming to be wise, they instead became utter fools. And instead of worshiping the glorious, ever-living God, they worshiped idols made to look like mere people and birds and animals and reptiles....They traded the truth about God for a lie.

—Rom. 1:18–23, 25

The Deception

Lucifer initiated the subversion in heaven. In the perfect environment of heaven, Lucifer was created.

> "You were the model of perfection,
>> full of wisdom and exquisite in beauty.
> You were in Eden,
>> the garden of God.
> Your clothing was adorned with every precious stone—
>> red carnelian, pale-green peridot, white moonstone,
>> blue-green beryl, onyx, green jasper,
>> blue lapis lazuli, turquoise, and emerald—
> all beautifully crafted for you
>> and set in the finest gold.
> They were given to you
>> on the day you were created."
>
> —Ezek. 28:12–13

Lucifer served in God's perfect presence. "I ordained and anointed you / as the mighty angelic guardian. / You had access to the holy mountain of God / and walked among the stones of fire" (Ezek. 28:14). But even in the perfect environment of heaven, in God's perfect presence, Lucifer believed he had a better plan than God. "Your heart was filled with pride / because of all your beauty. / Your wisdom was corrupted / by your love of splendor" (Ezek. 28:17).

> "How you are fallen from heaven,
>> O shining star, son of the morning!
> You have been thrown down to the earth,
>> you who destroyed the nations of the world.
> For you said to yourself,
>> 'I will ascend to heaven and set my throne above God's stars.

I will preside on the mountain of the gods
    far away in the north.
I will climb to the highest heavens
    and be like the Most High.'"

—Isa. 14:12–14

Lucifer perpetrated his faulty belief system that he should be god. He convinced one third of the angels that he had a better plan than God (Rev. 12:4). "So I banished you in disgrace / from the mountain of God. / I expelled you, O mighty guardian, / from your place among the stones of fire" (Ezek. 28:16).

Then God created the earth in splendor. In it He placed humanity for His pleasure. The story unfolds in Genesis. "Then the LORD God said, 'It is not good for the man to be alone. I will make a helper who is just right for him'" (2:18).

So the LORD God caused the man to fall into a deep sleep. While the man slept, the LORD God took out one of the man's ribs and closed up the opening. Then the LORD God made a woman from the rib, and He brought her to the man.
    "At last!" the man exclaimed.

"This one is bone from my bone,
    and flesh from my flesh!
She will be called 'woman,'
    because she was taken from 'man.'"

—Gen. 2:21–23

God's perfect design enjoyed harmony with the environment and the inhabitants. Adam and Eve relished their communion with each other and God as they walked in the cool of the day. The fellowship was sweet and the food was completely provided. God made provision for all man's needs. "Then God said, 'Look! I have given you every seed-bearing plant throughout the earth and all the fruit trees for your food. And I have given every green plant as food for all the wild animals, the birds in the sky, and the small animals that scurry along the ground—everything that has life.' And that is what happened" (1:29–30).

God even educated them about their responsibilities and established the government where His word was law. "The LORD God placed the man in the Garden of Eden to tend and watch over it. But the Lord God warned him, 'You may freely eat the fruit of every tree in the garden—except the tree of the knowledge of good and evil. If you eat its fruit, you are sure to die'" (2:15–17). As His significant creation, human beings were blessed and given the divine purpose to rule over His creation. "Then God blessed them and said, 'Be fruitful and multiply. Fill the earth and govern it. Reign over the fish in the sea, the birds in the sky, and all the animals that scurry along the ground'" (1:28).

It was very good.

The Distortion

Still believing he could be god, Satan devised a plan in an attempt to subvert God's design for humanity. By distorting Eve's view of God, the trap was laid for all humanity. Genesis 3 tells the story: "The serpent was the shrewdest of all the wild animals the Lord God had made. One day he asked the woman, 'Did God really say you must not eat the fruit from any of the trees in the garden?'" (3:1).

Perhaps the serpent feared he would be discovered if he honestly said what he wanted to: "Can't you see how God is depriving you? He made this beautiful fruit tree and won't even let you have any of it. He sure is selfish!"

> "Of course we may eat fruit from the trees in the garden," the woman replied. "It's only the fruit from the tree in the middle of the garden that we are not allowed to eat. God said, 'You must not eat it or even touch it; if you do, you will die.'"
> "You won't die!" the serpent replied to the woman.
>
> —Gen. 3:2–4

"God is being dishonest with you" was the underlying message the serpent conveyed. "God knows that your eyes will be opened as soon as you eat it, and you will be like God, knowing both good and evil" (3:5).

"The thing is God does not want you to be able to relate to Him. That's why He doesn't want you to eat of that fruit. He really doesn't want what's best for you. You shouldn't even trust Him." This was the serpent's subliminal implication.

Convinced God's plan was not the best plan for her, Eve decided to elect Satan as the ruler of the world. Her subversive plan became preeminent. God had created the world and established all that is, but it seemed He was depriving her. If she followed Satan's plan she could have more without God than she had by following God's law. Satan instilled within Eve a heightened sense of self, and then manipulated her into thinking she was not given adequate appreciation. Persuaded she was incomplete with God, Eve ate the fruit. "The woman was convinced. She saw that the tree was beautiful and its fruit looked delicious, and she wanted the wisdom it would give her. So she took some of the fruit and ate it. Then she gave some to her husband, who was with her, and he ate it, too" (3:6).

Every temptation that threatens us is a temptation to live independently from God. Believing God cannot be trusted to govern our lives as we see fit, we must complete ourselves—we must be god in our lives. This idolatrous belief perpetrates arrogance and selfish ambition as we follow our own way with a distorted view of God and reality.

Reality is based in God's absolute truth. If we don't see the way God does, it cannot be said that we are in reality. Therefore, we are living in delusion—a lie. The only power Satan has is the power of the lie. If we can get rid of the lies, we get rid of his power. "Satan has no authority or power over you except what you yield to him when you are deceived into believing his lies."[1] Few people live in reality. Most live in delusion based on lies.

But then the trauma of truth enters. With the choice to live independently of God, caustic consequences come to pass. Where there was once no shame, shame and guilt appear. "Now the man and his wife were both naked, but they felt no shame" (2:25).

For Adam and Eve, devising innovative solutions became their goal. "At that moment their eyes were opened, and they suddenly felt shame at their nakedness. So they sewed fig leaves together to cover themselves" (3:7). Profoundly altered as a result of their independent choices, Adam and Eve emerged possessing a different nature, manifesting a different character, and setting forth a different way of seeing life and experiencing God. No longer were they innocent before God. No longer were they in fellowship with God. No longer were they walking with God. Motivated by guilt, shame, and fear, Adam and Eve quickly collaborated to solve their dilemma: "How do we feel better about ourselves apart from God?" Innovation and creativity, once in service to God in naming the animals, produced the first line of designer clothing intended to cover their shame.

Delusions overrode reality, and they believed they could hide from God. "When the cool evening breezes were blowing, the man and his wife heard the LORD God walking about in the garden. So they hid from the LORD God among the trees" (3:8).

Fear and anxiety develop into a dominant way of life.

"Then the LORD God called to the man, 'Where are you?'

"He replied, 'I heard you walking in the garden, so I hid. I was afraid because I was naked'" (3:9–10).

Then the exploitive, evasive tactics were initiated. Attempting to control the situation while avoiding the truth, Adam started by blaming God. Eve passed the blame to the serpent.

> "Who told you that you were naked?" the LORD God asked. "Have you eaten from the tree whose fruit I commanded you not to eat?"
> The man replied, "It was the woman you gave me who gave me the fruit, and I ate it."
> Then the LORD God asked the woman, "What have you done?"
> "The serpent deceived me," she replied. "That's why I ate it."
>
> —Gen. 3:11–13

Blame and avoidance of personal responsibility are not new trends as we see in the garden encounter. There was a breakdown of interpersonal cohesion as the promotion and preservation of self emerged. In almost every personal and family crisis, we devise excuses and hypothesize explanations for wrongdoing as we seek to escape personal accountability.

In the 1960s the mantra was "The devil made me do it." Then in the 1970s and 80s, "Dad and Mom made me do it." Now, "DNA made me do it." Humanity blames religion, family, and biology to avoid personal accountability to God. In our attempts to evade responsibility, we are still weaving fig leaves and hiding behind trees as God calls out, "Where are you?"

To emerge from our bondage we must be willing to view our plight as intricately reflecting our personal sinfulness. Passing the blame does not remove any of the consequences. All receive a penalty.

> Then the LORD God said to the serpent,
>
> "Because you have done this, you are cursed
>   more than all animals, domestic and wild.
> You will crawl on your belly,
>   groveling in the dust as long as you live.
> And I will cause hostility between you and the woman,
>   and between your offspring and her offspring.
> He will strike your head,
>   and you will strike his heel."

Then he said to the woman,

"I will sharpen the pain of your pregnancy,
    and in pain you will give birth.
And you will desire to control your husband,
    but he will rule over you."

And to the man he said,

"Since you listened to your wife and ate from the tree
    whose fruit I commanded you not to eat,
the ground is cursed because of you.
    All your life you will struggle to scratch a living from it.
It will grow thorns and thistles for you,
    though you will eat of its grains.
By the sweat of your brow
    will you have food to eat
until you return to the ground
    from which you were made.
For you were made from dust,
    and to dust you will return."

—Gen. 3:14–19

As the story of Adam and Eve develops we witness the depression and anger that enter under the new government. They were expelled from the Garden of God to live in a world writhing in the pain of their consequences. "So the LORD God banished them from the Garden of Eden, and he sent Adam out to cultivate the ground from which he had been made" (3:23). "Against its will, all creation was subjected to God's curse. But with eager hope, the creation looks forward to the day when it will join God's children in glorious freedom from death and decay. For we know that all creation has been groaning as in the pains of childbirth right up to the present time" (Rom. 8:20–22).

The Disconnection

When Eve decided she wanted to complete the picture herself, she made a choice for all humanity throughout history. The serpent convinced her that the way God designed the portrait was lacking and that she could complete it better than the Creator. Satan became god of the world. "Satan, who is the god of this world, has blinded the minds of those who don't believe. They are unable to see the glorious light of the Good News. They don't understand this message about the glory of Christ, who is the exact likeness of God" (2 Cor. 4:4).

Spiritual death resulted from the choices Adam and Eve made. Their sin broke humanity's relationship with God, and the devastating consequences trouble us daily. As a result of the Garden encounter:

1. Humanity disconnected from truth and connected with perversion.
2. Humanity developed a distorted view of God's image.
3. Humanity created a delusional view of themselves.
4. Humanity began exploiting others for personal empowerment.
5. Humanity altered their purpose for living.

We are dominated by the negative emotions of shame, guilt, and fear, even while we search for love, joy, and peace. Because the world is not submitted to God's authority, insecurity invades the multiplicity of choices. Before the fall, the only choice that had to be made was to not eat of the tree! In our weak and helpless state we search for acceptance and a place to belong, but we experience only emptiness, futility, and turmoil.

But God still desires to be in a relationship with us. "Even before he made the world, God loved us and chose us in Christ to be holy and without fault in his eyes. God decided in advance to adopt us into his own family by bringing us to himself through Jesus Christ. This is what he wanted to do, and it gave him great pleasure" (Eph. 1:4–5).

Because of the sin that was passed to us, we are unable to be in a relationship with God. Violating God's law and usurping His authority requires a death penalty. "When Adam sinned, sin entered the world. Adam's sin brought death, so death spread to everyone, for everyone sinned" (Rom. 5:12). "For the wages of sin is death, but the free gift of God is eternal life through Christ Jesus our Lord" (Rom. 6:23).

Jesus Christ, the sinless Son of God, willingly became a human baby in order to pay the death penalty required on our behalf. Consider the sacrifice that was required to leave the throne of heaven to become a helpless baby! I cannot image reverting from an adult to an infant! How much more inconceivable to move from having all power and authority to having someone change your diapers!

We may agonize as we witness the cruel death He suffered. But the anguish of the cross can also be observed in another garden experience, the Garden of Gethsemane. "He took Peter and Zebedee's two sons, James and John, and he became anguished and distressed. He told them, 'My soul is crushed with grief to the point of death. Stay here and keep watch with me'" (Matt. 26:37–38).

> He walked away, about a stone's throw, and knelt down and prayed, "Father, if you are willing, please take this cup of suffering away from me. Yet I want your will to be done, not mine." Then an angel from heaven appeared and strengthened him. He prayed more fervently, and he was in such agony of spirit that his sweat fell to the ground like great drops of blood.
>
> —Luke 22:41–44

Jesus knew that when He became sin for us, His Father would not be able to be in a relationship with Him for that point in time, because God can have no part with sin. The crisis of the cross was that Christ had to face the penalty of sin without God. So glibly we pummel through our day, striving to be independent, inconsiderate of the consequences. But Jesus knew the horror of facing even one minute without a relationship to God. He modeled a life that was totally dependent on God. The trauma of the tragedy was that He willingly sacrificed His relationship with the Father in order to be in a relationship with you and me!

> So we praise God for the glorious grace he has poured out on us who belong to his dear Son. He is so rich in kindness and grace that he purchased our freedom with the blood of his Son and forgave our sins. He has showered his kindness on us, along with all wisdom and understanding.
>
> God has now revealed to us his mysterious plan regarding Christ, a plan to fulfill his own good pleasure. And this is the plan: At the right time he will bring everything together under the authority of Christ—everything in heaven and on earth. Furthermore,

because we are united with Christ, we have received an inheritance from God, for he chose us in advance, and he makes everything work out according to his plan.

—Eph. 1:6–11

Christ's sacrifice does not automatically bring us into a relationship with God. Like Adam and Eve, we are faced with a choice: Who will be God of my world? By default Satan is the god of this evil world, but by choice God can take the throne in your life. You are free to make the choice to continue in your independence or to choose to live a life that is desperately dependent on God.

With our own fate in our hands, we fall for the same distortions that deceived Adam and Eve. Even one third of the angels in the perfect environment of heaven believed the cunning lies of Lucifer. The movie *The Jungle Book* depicts Kaa the snake hypnotizing Mowgli while he stealthily wraps his coils to suffocate the unsuspecting victim. How often is that scene replayed as Satan deceives us into believing that our will is superior to God's? We embrace the perversion over truth, while we demote God and promote ourselves as the authority.

"For you are the children of your father the devil, and you love to do the evil things he does. He was a murderer from the beginning. He has always hated the truth, because there is no truth in him. When he lies, it is consistent with his character; for he is a liar and the father of lies" (John 8:44).

In talking about our portrait of God, Michael Easley states, "It radically affects the way we see God seeing us. If we don't have a clear theology of who God is and how we envision Him, then we're not going to have a clear view of who we are before God and how we should then live."[2] How do you view God? If asked, "Do you have a distorted view of God?" most likely you would promptly respond, "No, I do not have a distorted view of God. I love the Lord. I know He loves me. I trust Him. And I do not know what I would do without Him." But if you were asked, "Have you worried this week?" More than likely you would have to confess, "Yes, I have." What does your worry say you believe about God? The answer may consist of responses such as "I don't believe God will take care of me"; "God does not have my best interests in mind"; "I do not trust that God will do things my way." Responses such as these indicate you have distorted views of God that shape your understanding of how God will interact with you. As we live within our distorted views of God, our hearts are molded according to the likeness of our distortions, motivating us to live independently of God.

How can we know what we believe about God? The Bible teaches that our behaviors reveal our hearts. In Matthew's gospel, Jesus taught His disciples how to discern the difference between the real prophet of God and those who are deceivers.

> Beware of false prophets who come disguised as harmless sheep but are really vicious wolves. You can identify them by their fruit, that is, by the way they act. Can you pick grapes from thornbushes, or figs from thistles? A good tree produces good fruit, and a bad tree produces bad fruit. A good tree can't produce bad fruit, and a bad tree can't produce good fruit. So every tree that does not produce good fruit is chopped down and thrown into the fire. Yes, just as you can identify a tree by its fruit, so you can identify people by their actions.
>
> —Matt. 7:15–20

Jesus teaches that behaviors reveal the soul as easily as a tree is known by its fruit.

To obtain a clearer picture of how you view God, ask yourself this question: Based on my behavior, what do I believe about God? For example, "Based on my overindulgence with food, alcohol, drugs, etc., what do I believe about God?" Answer: "I believe I cannot be complete in Christ." "So what do I believe about myself?" "I believe I can be complete through my own efforts." Try another one: "Based on my behavior of only praying when there is a crisis, what do I believe about God?" Answer: "I believe He is only helpful in a crisis." "What do I believe about myself?" "I believe I can handle life on my own, except for a crisis."

Behavior is a direct descendent of belief that reveals the condition of the soul. Mark adds to Matthew's narrative by emphasizing the reason the behavior can reveal the heart—the heart establishes the behavior.

> And then he added, "It is what comes from inside that defiles you. For from within, out of a person's heart, come evil thoughts, sexual immorality, theft, murder, adultery, greed, wickedness, deceit, lustful desires, envy, slander, pride, and foolishness. All these vile things come from within; they are what defile you."
>
> —Mark 7:20–23

You may be traumatized to realize that you have been deceived even as Eve and Adam were. Satan continues his cunning ploys because they have been successful through the ages. And so we still fall for the lie that we can live independently of God while disregarding the fact that "In the beginning God created the heavens and the earth" (Gen. 1:1). God created all that is. He has the best ideas on how all things work together. Why should we believe we could come up with a better idea than God about how anything should operate?

Insight Journal

For this Insight Journal, prayerfully consider at least five behaviors that characterize your life. To obtain a clearer picture of how you view God, ask yourself these questions concerning each of your behaviors:

Based on my behavior, what do I believe about God?
  Based on my behavior, what do I believe about myself?
For certain behaviors it may also be relevant to ask the following:
  Based on my behavior, what do I believe about others?
  Based on my behavior, what do I believe about my reason for living?

Behavior 1
Based on my behavior, what do I believe about God?
  Based on my behavior, what do I believe about myself?
Based on my behavior, what do I believe about others?
  Based on my behavior, what do I believe about my reason for living?

Behaviors 2–5
Based on my behavior, what do I believe about God?
  Based on my behavior, what do I believe about myself?
Based on my behavior, what do I believe about others?
  Based on my behavior, what do I believe about my reason for living?

(See appendix C: Bad Belief/Good God for additional insights.)

Psalms Prayer Pattern

Keep me safe, O God,
  for I have come to you for refuge.

I said to the LORD, "You are my Master!
  Every good thing I have comes from you."
The godly people in the land
  are my true heroes!
  I take pleasure in them!
Troubles multiply for those who chase after other gods.
  I will not take part in their sacrifices of blood
  or even speak the names of their gods.

LORD, you alone are my inheritance, my cup of blessing.
  You guard all that is mine.
The land you have given me is a pleasant land.
  What a wonderful inheritance!

I will bless the LORD who guides me;
  even at night my heart instructs me.
I know the LORD is always with me.
  I will not be shaken, for he is right beside me.

No wonder my heart is glad, and I rejoice.
  My body rests in safety.
For you will not leave my soul among the dead
  or allow your holy one to rot in the grave.
You will show me the way of life,
  granting me the joy of your presence
  and the pleasures of living with you forever.

—Ps. 16

PART 2

The Solution—Christ Is Relevant

CHAPTER 6

The Truth about God

WHILE VIEWING THE portrait of God, our perceptions become perverted by the lens of Satan's lies. "You used to live in sin, just like the rest of the world, obeying the devil—the commander of the powers in the unseen world. He is the spirit at work in the hearts of those who refuse to obey God" (Eph. 2:2). "But whenever someone turns to the Lord, the veil is taken away. For the Lord is the Spirit, and wherever the Spirit of the Lord is, there is freedom. So all of us who have had that veil removed can see and reflect the glory of the Lord. And the Lord—who is the Spirit—makes us more and more like him as we are changed into his glorious image" (2 Cor. 3:16–18).

With "the knowledge of God and of Jesus our Lord" (2 Peter 1:2 KJV) as our firm foundation, God establishes three pillars of Christianity that provide a stable structure for our lives. These truths affect how we encounter, embrace, and experience God as we mature in our relationship with Christ:

- God is real; therefore He is relevant.
- God is love; therefore He is compassionate.
- God is sovereign; therefore He is trustworthy.

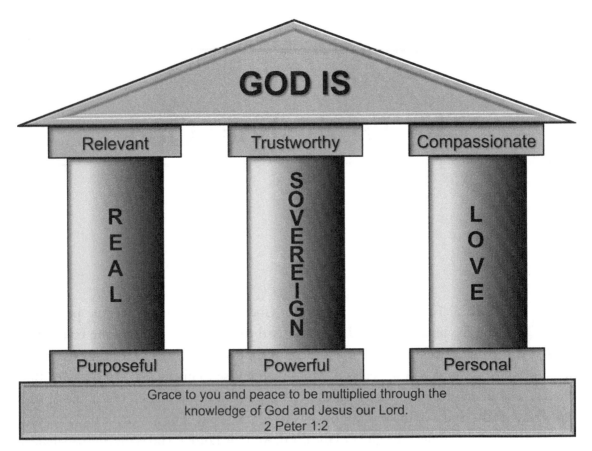

Three Pillars of Christianity

God Is Real, Therefore He Is Relevant

God desires an intimate relationship with His creation. He is not merely an impersonal creator who has left His creation to fend for itself. He is a real God who desires humanity to experience Him as relevant to every aspect of life. John spoke of the joy that results when we encounter Christ as real and relevant.

We proclaim to you the one who existed from the beginning, whom we have heard and seen. We saw him with our own eyes and touched him with our own hands. He is the Word of life. This one who is life itself was revealed to us, and we have seen him. And now we testify and proclaim to you that he is the one who is eternal life. He was with the Father, and then he was revealed to us. We proclaim to you what we ourselves have actually seen and heard so that you may have fellowship with us. And our fellowship is with the Father and with his Son, Jesus Christ. We are writing these things so that you may fully share our joy.

—1 John 1:1–4

Webster's dictionary defines *relevant* as "having significant and demonstrable bearing on the matter at hand; affording evidence tending to prove or disprove the matter at issue or under discussion."[1] Is there significant and demonstrable evidence that God is real in your life? If we say we believe God is real, then His reality will be reflected as we demonstrate His image in our lives. As we daily experience God as relevant, our lives offer proof of His existence to a watching world. There must always be an interaction between what we profess and what our lives evidence. The essence of Christianity is not mere profession of faith, but rather possession of faith, where the truth of Christ is confirmed by the reality of our lives.

Jesus Christ demonstrated God's reality and relevance when He paid the price for our sins. "The Son radiates God's own glory and expresses the very character of God, and he sustains everything by the mighty power of his command. When he had cleansed us from our sins, he sat down in the place of honor at the right hand of the majestic God in heaven" (Heb. 1:3).

"Do you believe God is real?" The question is not asking if you know *about* God, if you know *of* God, or even if you have been educated concerning God. The question asks, is Jesus relevant, pertinent, and applicable in your life? Does He make a difference?

One day as I (Kirk) sat in my office, I was feeling particularly powerless, vulnerable, inadequate, and worthless. In my desperation I began to pray, "God, be real to me. Show me Your power. I need to experience You as real." Truthfully, I did not anticipate the response I encountered from God. The Holy Spirit promptly said to my heart and mind, "The issue of My reality is not in question. Look at the birds, trees, and all of creation, even the fish in your aquarium. Do they not declare My glory? Why then do you say to Me, 'Be real to me?' I am as real as I am ever going to be! The issue at hand is not My being real to you, but when will you be real with Me?" I could not be aware of God's relevance in my life until I was real with God.

Operating under the guise of submission, we petition God to make a difference in our lives. But when His Spirit speaks to reveal His plan, we continue on our own way, pretending not to hear His guidance. "Come on, get real!" Do you really want what God wants, or do you just *say* you want what He wants? When we assert that we want God to be ruler in our lives, we must become real with God by implementing the plan He has laid before us. Unless we are willing to employ His resources, we will never experience Him in a relevant manner.

We run from God's truth in our lives. We do not listen for God's guidance, or we pretend not to hear. He tries to wake us from our stupor with warning signals such as anxiety, but we employ a variety of evasive tactics as we attempt to squelch His truth from our listening souls. Until we are willing to acknowledge His plan of truth, God will continue waiting for us while we continue to miss Him.

We want to meet with God on our terms, but He will meet us only on His terms. We want to relate with Him in a way that is comfortable to us, but anything short of God's plan is a deception. We forfeit reality for comfort and give up a relevant encounter with God.

The Bible uses the term *confess* to identify the juncture where we become congruent with the mind of God regarding His revealed truth. God asks us to confess foundational truths such as Jesus Christ is the Son of God and Lord (1 John 4:15; Rom. 10:9), Jesus is relevant (Luke 12:8), and we are sinful (1 John 1:9). Confession is key to an authentic relationship with God. As we become congruent with God's description of us and our sin, we no longer succumb to Satan's deceptions that keep us bound. When we confront the truth about ourselves, we agree with God that He is the only one capable of delivering us. We are incapable of living an independent life.

Under the pretext of spirituality we miss a relevant relationship with Jesus. Christ asserted to His disciples that a true relationship with Him is more than just performing good deeds, even if they do appear to be supernatural and miraculous. "On judgment day many will say to me, 'Lord! Lord! We prophesied in your name and cast out demons in your name and performed many miracles in your name.' But I will reply, 'I never knew you. Get away from me, you who break God's laws'" (Matt. 7:22–23).

"These people honor me with their lips, / but their hearts are far from me. / Their worship is a farce, / for they teach man-made ideas as commands from God" (Matt. 15:8–9).

Jesus favors a simple childlike trust when we enter into reliance upon Him, fostering a dependent connection with Him through truth. Placing our faith in all Christ has revealed to us about Himself, and confessing to Him all He has revealed to us about ourselves moves us to authentically encounter Him, to actually know Him, and to be known by Him.

God, through Jesus Christ is relevant to our lives when

- He is our reason for living.
  I live because of the living Father who sent me; in the same way, anyone who feeds on me will live because of me (John 6:57).

- He is our resource for thriving.
  The Spirit alone gives eternal life. Human effort accomplishes nothing. And the very words I have spoken to you are spirit and life (John 6:63).

- He is our resolution to crisis.
  We were crushed and overwhelmed beyond our ability to endure, and we thought we would never live through it. In fact, we expected to die. But as a result, we stopped relying on ourselves and learned to rely only on God, who raises the dead (2 Cor. 1:8–9).

God Is Love, Therefore He Is Compassionate

One of my (Melanie) earliest childhood memories recalls pumping my legs passionately to swing to the clouds while singing, "Yes, Jesus Loves Me." This elementary song saturated my soul, but even in adulthood it is difficult to comprehend the depths of that simple truth.

"When we were utterly helpless, Christ came at just the right time and died for us sinners. Now, most people would not be willing to die for an upright person, though someone might perhaps be willing to die for a person who is especially good. But God showed his great love for us by sending Christ to die for us while we were still sinners" (Rom. 5:6–8).

Can anything ever separate us from Christ's love? Does it mean he no longer loves us if we have trouble or calamity, or are persecuted, or hungry, or destitute, or in danger, or threatened with death?…No, despite all these things, overwhelming victory is ours through Christ, who loved us.

And I am convinced that nothing can ever separate us from God's love. Neither death nor life, neither angels nor demons, neither our fears for today nor our worries about tomorrow—not even the powers of hell can separate us from God's love. No power in the sky above or in the earth below—indeed, nothing in all creation will ever be able to separate us from the love of God that is revealed in Christ Jesus our Lord.

—Rom. 8:35–39

The truth of God's love is not just a fact; it becomes a reality when we can recognize that because God loves us, He cares about every area of our lives. Not only does He care, but He also understands our deepest struggles, and He desires to be the solution for our every problem.

"This High Priest of ours [Jesus] understands our weaknesses, for he faced all of the same testing we do, yet he did not sin. So let us come boldly to the throne of our gracious God. There we will receive his mercy, and we will find grace to help us when we need it most" (Heb. 4:15–16).

Erroneously we believe the deception that if God really does love us and really does care, He would make everything easy with smooth sailing. How can crisis and tribulation be evidence of a loving God? But even God's gift of love to us required grief, agony, and despair. "For God so loved the world that He gave His only begotten Son, that whoever believes in Him should not perish but have everlasting life" (John 3:16 NKJV).

On a particularly desperate day, the simple fact of God's love for me (Kirk) became a powerful, relevant truth. Submitting to lifetime ministry did not isolate us from crisis and tribulation. The fiery darts of the wicked one inundated us with unrelenting force. The battle was fierce. It was the kind of spiritual warfare that challenged every fiber of my being.

As I was driving en route to pay a bill, I looked up and said to God in the privacy of my truck, "Lord, I'm at my end. I think I'm finished. There is nothing left in me to carry on. I don't have anything else to give." I was beaten. I had no more stamina. No more ability to endure. I was not depressed; I did not want to die. I was, however, pressed beyond my measure to continue the fight. I was exhausted.

"God,…I am finished! I don't know what will become of me or how I will continue into tomorrow. God, unless You do something, it's over for me." My prayer to God was as tired and devoid of emotion as it could have ever been and still be articulated. All I could do was to look to God and say, "Please help me."

God had me right where He wanted me. It was at this broken place I received from God the greatest gift I could ever have—His love! I have placed this event in the annals of the most significant experiences with God I have ever had.

God's Spirit opened my mind that day to all verses of Scripture, sermons, and songs I have ever read, preached, heard preached, or sung, testifying to His great love for me. I began to be flooded with the love of Christ beyond anything I have ever known or thought was possible. His nurturing was powerful and tangible; I could feel His presence. As I was being cocooned within His love, the peace of God surpassed my understanding while I was serenaded by the very songs of how much He loves me. All my worries, my fears, my concerns for life, and how I would make it past today were enraptured in the vortex of His person. I was now strengthened with His might. It was at this moment that I wanted nothing more than what God wanted for me.

Immediately I began to sob from the depths of my soul, the apathy now vanquished. My tears flowed in praise to my God, my Deliverer, my Lord and Savior, who really, truly loves me. These tears of praise continued for hours. I sobbed until the sobbing could no longer be sustained. Then I would sob some more. That day I was rejuvenated by the hand of God and taught that I could live only through His power. It became clear to me: I must see Jesus as relevant to all areas of my life; I must understand that He cares about every area of my life. I have never forgotten this, nor have I ever been the same.

"Then Jesus said, 'Come to me, all of you who are weary and carry heavy burdens, and I will give you rest. Take my yoke upon you. Let me teach you, because I am humble and gentle at heart, and you will find rest for your souls. For my yoke is easy to bear, and the burden I give you is light'" (Matt. 11:28–30).

"Listen to me, descendants of Jacob,
    all you who remain in Israel.
I have cared for you since you were born.
    Yes, I carried you before you were born.
I will be your God throughout your lifetime—
    until your hair is white with age.
I made you, and I will care for you.
    I will carry you along and save you."

—Isa. 46:3–4

God Is Sovereign, Therefore He Is Trustworthy

God is sovereign. His domain, power, and authority are unparalleled and unrivaled. There is no restraint or inhibition placed on Him that prevents the exercise of His will. God is without limits and needs no permission to act. Guided only by His personal attributes, He rules over all. God knows the beginning and the end of time, and sees into eternity as if it were today.

We are inclined to interpret God's sovereignty as a concept akin to control; and we therefore assign expectations, anticipating protection from harassment, hurt, and harm. We then look forward to being prospered exponentially by being healthy, wealthy, and wise. However, God's sovereignty is not accomplished through His being controlling; nor is it synonymous with control. God is sovereign but not controlling. We have trouble conceptualizing how God could be all-powerful and over all if He does not control all.

Control implies the necessity for others to cooperate in order for something to be brought to completion. Intimidation is also implied, insinuating that there is someone or something able to overpower the threatening interest. God accomplishes His plans regardless of any willing cooperation. He possesses ultimate authority over all the kings of the earth, the devils that roam the earth, and the will of humans upon the earth. But God does not need to control any of these interests to perform His plan. Therefore God can allow all to have free will, and still His plans will come to fruition.

People are very uncomfortable with the concept of God's sovereignty. The idea of God acting solely according to His plan often provokes fear. Instead, we would rather He be controlling, or better yet controllable. Believing that an all-powerful, all-knowing, always-present God can be influenced to accomplish what *we* want produces much comfort and presents great appeal. If God can be an extension of my control, this elicits much motivation to beseech Him. Yet it is an erroneous understanding and has been the impetus for much criticism that God has let us down.

Truly it is impossible for the human mind to fully comprehend the concept of God's sovereignty. With our limited insight we attempt to justify all the ramifications, but the ways of God are past finding out.

Oh, how great are God's riches and wisdom and knowledge! How impossible it is for us to understand his decisions and his ways!

For who can know the LORD's thoughts?
    Who knows enough to give him advice?
And who has given him so much
    that he needs to pay it back?

For everything comes from him and exists by his power and is intended for his glory. All glory to him forever! Amen.

—Rom. 11:33–36

The most frequently asked question by both the hurting of heart and the skeptical of soul is "Why does God allow people to suffer?" God is certainly moved by our infirmities, but He is not controlled by them. This is illustrated in Paul's own prayer for healing.

Three different times I begged the Lord to take it [the thorn in my flesh] away. Each time he said, "My grace is all you need. My power works best in weakness." So now I am glad to boast about my weaknesses, so that the power of Christ can work through me. That's why I take pleasure in my weaknesses, and in the insults, hardships, persecutions, and troubles that I suffer for Christ. For when I am weak, then I am strong.

—2 Cor. 12:8–10

So, "Why does God allow people to suffer?" The honest intent of this question fails to understand the context in which we live. God is sovereign, but He does not have jurisdiction over the earth. God respects the authority of Satan's claim to the earth given to him by the sin of Adam and Eve. Their vote to usurp God's authority in favor of Satan's deception entitled him to rule the world. This effectively placed humanity under the domain of evil, and therefore we are daily affected by evil even to the point of abuse.

The Bible refers to Satan in succinct terms as "the god of this world" (2 Cor. 4:4), and "the prince of the power of the air, the spirit that is now working in the sons of disobedience" (Eph. 2:2 NASB). James, the half-brother of Jesus added, "Let no one say when he is tempted, 'I am being tempted by God'; for God cannot be tempted by evil, and He Himself does not tempt anyone. But each one is tempted when he is carried away and enticed by his own lust. Then when lust has conceived, it gives birth to sin; and when sin is accomplished, it brings forth death" (James 1:13–15 NASB).

Satan's dominion extends only to the unredeemed aspect of this world, which at this point is everything except the church. The church, though not *of* the world, is *in* the world, and is therefore subject to harassment, hurt, and harm from the ungodly element. Paul testified that God had commissioned him "...to open their eyes so that they may turn from darkness to light and from the dominion of Satan to God, that they may receive forgiveness of sins and an inheritance among those who have been sanctified by faith in Me" (Acts 26:18 NASB).

God allows people to be touched by evil because He is capable of redeeming them from it. As God's dominion is expanded through evangelism and His interests are advanced by disciple making, the more evil will be restrained and the innocent protected. Then we will witness the fulfillment of the biblical admonition, "Don't let evil conquer you, but conquer evil by doing good" (Rom. 12:21).

Scripture asserts that people suffer because this world is ruled by Satan, dominated by sin, and because sinful people do sinful things. All the carnage in this world that is often attributed to God can be traced back to the origin of evil present and at large in the world today. Yet our sovereign God remains connected; He has in no way been ousted by Satan. Satan was defeated at the cross, but his final consequences have not yet taken effect. In time he will be removed.

"Nevertheless you will be thrust down to Sheol [hell],
To the recesses of the pit.
Those who see you will gaze at you,
They will ponder over you, saying,
'Is this the man who made the earth tremble,
Who shook kingdoms,
Who made the world like a wilderness
And overthrew its cities,
Who did not allow his prisoners to go home?'"

—Isa. 14:15–17 NASB

God's sovereignty promises that when we encounter the evil of this world we will be encompassed by the love, mercy, and grace of God to the perfecting of our souls, the performing of God's will, and the proclaiming of His faithfulness. Therefore, it is imperative for us to believe "...that God causes all things to work together for good to those who love Him, to those who are called according to His purpose" (Rom. 8:28 NASB).

"For I am confident of this very thing, that He who began a good work in you will perfect it until the day of Christ Jesus" (Phil. 1:6 NASB).

All He is accomplishing in our simple lives is for the purpose of establishing a deeper relationship with Him so that we may evidence Christ's work.

> We now have this light shining in our hearts, but we ourselves are like fragile clay jars containing this great treasure. This makes it clear that our great power is from God, not from ourselves.
>
> We are pressed on every side by troubles, but we are not crushed. We are perplexed, but not driven to despair. We are hunted down, but never abandoned by God. We get knocked down, but we are not destroyed. Through suffering, our bodies continue to share in the death of Jesus so that the life of Jesus may also be seen in our bodies.
>
> —2 Cor. 4:7–10

God is real, God is love, and God is sovereign; therefore, He is relevant, He is compassionate, and He is worthy of our trust. All who have given themselves to Him in brokenness, repentance, submission, and obedience benefit from His transforming power that is conforming us to His image. The fruit of His Spirit emerges as our own personal attributes reflect the fact that Jesus Christ is at work, faithfully keeping His promises.

> His divine power has granted to us everything pertaining to life and godliness, through the true knowledge of Him who called us by His own glory and excellence. For by these He has granted to us His precious and magnificent promises, so that by them you may become partakers of the divine nature, having escaped the corruption that is in the world by lust.
>
> —2 Peter 1:3–4 NASB

Insight Journal

1. Children see God as relevant because they can trust that there is someone bigger who knows the best way to make things work out. When did I lose that concept of God?
2. What evidence is there in my life that God is real?
3. I know God loves me because … (try to make an extensive list, not just a preprogrammed answer)
4. I can trust God because …
5. Do I really want what God wants, or do I just *say* I want what He wants? I am afraid to want what God wants for me because …

Psalms Prayer Pattern

O Lord, you have examined my heart
  and know everything about me.
You know when I sit down or stand up.
  You know my thoughts even when I'm far away.
You see me when I travel
  and when I rest at home.
  You know everything I do.
You know what I am going to say
  even before I say it, Lord.
You go before me and follow me.
  You place your hand of blessing on my head.
Such knowledge is too wonderful for me,
  too great for me to understand!

I can never escape from your Spirit!
  I can never get away from your presence!
If I go up to heaven, you are there;
  if I go down to the grave, you are there.
If I ride the wings of the morning,
  if I dwell by the farthest oceans,
even there your hand will guide me,
  and your strength will support me.
I could ask the darkness to hide me
  and the light around me to become night—
  but even in darkness I cannot hide from you.
To you the night shines as bright as day.
  Darkness and light are the same to you.

You made all the delicate, inner parts of my body
  and knit me together in my mother's womb.
Thank you for making me so wonderfully complex!
  Your workmanship is marvelous—how well I know it.

You watched me as I was being formed in utter seclusion,
    as I was woven together in the dark of the womb.
You saw me before I was born.
    Every day of my life was recorded in your book.
Every moment was laid out
    before a single day had passed.

How precious are your thoughts about me, O God.
    They cannot be numbered!
I can't even count them;
    they outnumber the grains of sand!
And when I wake up,
    you are still with me!

O God, if only you would destroy the wicked!
    Get out of my life, you murderers!
They blaspheme you;
    your enemies misuse your name.
O Lord, shouldn't I hate those who hate you?
    Shouldn't I despise those who oppose you?
Yes, I hate them with total hatred,
    for your enemies are my enemies.

Search me, O God, and know my heart;
    test me and know my anxious thoughts.
Point out anything in me that offends you,
    and lead me along the path of everlasting life.

—Ps. 139

CHAPTER 7

What Is God's Job in My Life?

ANOTHER CHILDHOOD ADVENTURE invited us to search for hidden treasures. With coded map in hand we attempted to calculate the incomprehensible wealth that could be obtained if we deciphered all the cryptic symbols. Movies depicting desolate caverns filled with overflowing coffers fueled our lust for all that is tantalizing.

Somewhere along our journey we came to believe that our dreams could be satisfied by God; He would give us everything we wanted if we could just decipher all the cryptic symbols. The good news is that Christ has provided an incomprehensible treasure, but it is a treasure of His design, not necessarily a fulfillment of our wishes.

Genesis recounts the story of how the treasure was lost. Beginning in the Garden of Eden, humanity purposed to reclaim the lost treasure but continuously sought for fleeting satisfaction rather than the ultimate treasure. Even in the garden God provided the clues that would lead to His abundant storehouse, and the way was revealed by the cross.

The work of the cross enables us to inherit the riches of Christ if we accept His work on our behalf. "His divine power has granted to us everything pertaining to life and godliness" (2 Peter 1:3 NASB). His coffers overflow with abundant provision sufficient for every need, as we are being conformed to the image of Jesus Christ. A divine treasure spills over with inexhaustible wealth awaiting acquisition, and as God's children we are heirs to His vast treasure. A closer look at 2 Peter 1 gives a definitive outline of the work that has already been done and the treasures that await those who diligently seek Him. God is our Savior, sustainer, and benefactor.

Savior

God calls us to Himself because He loves us and desires an intimate and personal relationship with us. The righteous work of Jesus Christ provides the opportunity for us to choose salvation that results in communion with God.

"To those who have obtained like precious faith with us by the righteousness of our God and Savior Jesus Christ" (2 Peter 1:1 NKJV). Jesus Christ pleased the Father by being the acceptable sacrifice in our place. Our sin natures separated us from a relationship with God, but Jesus did everything necessary to make the way for us to come to God. It is His work that makes us acceptable to God, not any particular formula of human design. Erroneously we believe it is our responsibility to appease God and become acceptable to Him. Perhaps we assume that by doing the right thing, saying the right thing, or doing "it" good enough we can gain entrance into a relationship with God. Some even suppose they are entitled to access to God because of their upright lifestyle. The two polar extremes that block dependency on Jesus are "I am not good enough" and "I am good enough." The reality is that it is not about us—whether we are or are not good enough. It is about Christ and what He has accomplished. When we come to salvation, we are choosing to depend and rely on God in all areas of our lives. "He died for everyone so that those who receive his new life will no longer live for themselves. Instead, they will live for Christ, who died and was raised for them" (2 Cor. 5:15).

It pleased the Father to provide for our best interest through His redemptive work.

All praise to God, the Father of our Lord Jesus Christ. It is by his great mercy that we have been born again, because God raised Jesus Christ from the dead. Now we live with great expectation, and we have a priceless inheritance—an inheritance that is kept in heaven for you, pure and undefiled, beyond the reach of change and decay. And through your faith, God is protecting you by his power until you receive this salvation, which is ready to be revealed on the last day for all to see.

—1 Peter 1:3–5

God's undeserved, limitless grace is available to address the core needs of the soul. Christ offers

- Redemption from the
  - Domain of Satan
  - Domination of sin
  - Damnation to hell
  - Dictates of this present evil world
- Resolution of
  - Guilt
  - Shame
  - Fear
- Restoration to
  - Love
  - Joy
  - Peace
- Reconciliation
  - To God
  - Through Jesus
  - By the Holy Spirit

God looks into our lives and considers the trials and difficulties He foresees will come to us. He has already designed a master plan of how He will navigate us through the maze of trouble to ensure our arrival at His preordained destination. "For God knew his people in advance, and he chose them to become like his Son, so that his Son would be the firstborn among many brothers and sisters" (Rom. 8:29).

God deals with us right where we are, using the circumstances and problems we face to move us toward the likeness of Christ. God's dynamic transforming process is set in motion through His grace as we act on His truth.

We also pray that you will be strengthened with all his glorious power so you will have all the endurance and patience you need. May you be filled with joy, always thanking the Father. He has enabled you to share in the inheritance that belongs to his people, who live in the light. For he has rescued us from the kingdom of darkness and transferred us into the Kingdom of his dear Son, who purchased our freedom and forgave our sins.

—Col. 1:11–14

God calls His children, and chooses all those who are willing to choose Him.

Even before he made the world, God loved us and chose us in Christ to be holy and without fault in his eyes. God decided in advance to adopt us into his own family by bringing us to himself through Jesus Christ. This is what he wanted to do, and it gave him great pleasure. So we praise God for the glorious grace he has poured out on us who belong to his dear Son. He is so rich in kindness and grace that he purchased our freedom with the blood of his Son and forgave our sins. He has showered his kindness on us, along with all wisdom and understanding.

—Eph. 1:4–8

As our Savior He purposed to free us from the bondage of sin that keeps us stuck in the mire. His gracious action was prompted by His eternal desire to be in an intimate relationship with His creation. The resulting freedom and union enables His child to live devoted to God and totally committed to doing good deeds.

For the grace of God has been revealed, bringing salvation to all people. And we are instructed to turn from godless living and sinful pleasures. We should live in this evil world with wisdom, righteousness, and devotion to God, while we look forward with hope to that wonderful day when the glory of our great God and Savior, Jesus Christ, will be revealed. He gave his life to free us from every kind of sin, to cleanse us, and to make us his very own people, totally committed to doing good deeds.

—Titus 2:11–14

Sustainer

The extent of God's blessings does not stop with the discovery of the divine treasure of salvation, for within the celestial cavern glows the continuing grace of God through Jesus Christ our Sustainer. Grace, practically understood, is the power to live supplied by God. Jesus literally gives us the capacity to live beyond ourselves. Specifically, He enables us to live beyond our fleshly abilities to be empowered by His divine nature. When our feeble flesh cries, "I can't do this," we can reach for His supply of grace and recognize that we do not have to face any issue in life with our meager capabilities. "Then call on me when you are in trouble, / and I will rescue you, / and you will give me glory" (Ps. 50:15).

As a three-and-a-half-year-old boy, I (Kirk) remember carrying water during a drought in a galvanized bucket from a spring across the dirt road where we lived in rural North Carolina. I recall using both arms and bumping the heavy pail full of water from side to side between my legs. While water sloshed out onto the ground behind me, Mama said, "Honey, there won't be any water left by the time we get home." Still, I was determined to carry the water. I wanted to be strong like Daddy. My hands hurt as the old metal handle dug into my palms. The bucket dragged the ground, providing temporary relief as my hands swelled with pain. But we still had not crossed the road.

Then came the unexpected. From somewhere behind me with a singular motion my dad swooped his little boy onto his shoulders while he shifted my load into his large, strong hands. With both my trembling hands I desperately grasped his jet-black hair. I was terrified, I was thrilled, and I was on top of the world. Though only three-and-a-half years old I now possessed all the power of my father. I was living beyond myself, beyond my capabilities. I was now walking in the awesome power of my dad. No longer did I need to struggle to accomplish my task; I merely had to rest in his strength.

The Scriptures teach that God is actively working to bring His children to completeness and fulfillment. The Christian's life is abuzz with divine activity. Jesus is constantly involved with His disciples to bring each one to maturity, "until we all attain to the unity of the faith, and of the knowledge of the Son of God, to a mature man, to the measure of the stature which belongs to the fullness of Christ" (Eph. 4:13 NASB). Grace is the all-encompassing biblical concept used to depict the process that starts with salvation and ends with perfecting us into the image of Jesus Christ.

The prospect of God's unmerited favor giving undeserving people the power to live depends exclusively upon the person of Christ. Jesus provided the way to access God so we can have the power to live the life He lived in the fashion in which He lived it—being dependent upon God. Grace is the catalyst, providing what is needed and furnishing what is lacking to embed the image of Jesus Christ, God's most precious treasure, on our souls.

God anticipates every challenge, while enabling us through His grace to have the power to live Jesus' life on earth. All His spiritual, psychological, and interpersonal power that is beyond our comprehension and aptitude is made user-friendly through God's truth in our lives. We are not required to have a thorough understanding of the inner workings of God's abilities, nor a profound knowledge of the intricacies of our problems. It is sufficient to know, "I am hurting"; "I am afraid"; or "I am sinking"; and that God is able to rescue me from this present evil world as I desperately depend upon Jesus Christ. A desperate dependency on Jesus reveals God's abundant power: "The Lord is close to the brokenhearted; / he rescues those whose spirits are crushed" (Ps. 34:18).

Jesus addresses the needs of our hearts through enlightenment, drawing directly from His principles, precepts, and promises concerning Himself, thereby aiding His children to experience Him as relevant to the needs of their human condition. God works without ceasing to provide us with His grace.

The prize of peace is the logical outcome of God's grace as asserted in 2 Peter 1:2 (NET): "May grace and peace be lavished on you as you grow in the rich knowledge of God and of Jesus our Lord!"

Grace from heaven moves the heart to calm tranquility. When our core needs are addressed, the issue of well-being is resolved, the crisis of the day is settled, the intricacies of interpersonal relations are solved, and the prospect of pleasing God is complete, God's peace pervades. When will that ever happen? When we access God's grace. The provision has already been made for us to experience His grace, but we must receive it. God has already done His job.

To access God's affluence, entrance must be gained through the knowledge of God and of Jesus our Lord. God has provided the knowledge, but it falls to us to believe His truth. The abundance of grace and peace multiplies as we connect to the truth about Jesus and then apply this knowledge to our circumstances and situations. The application and experience of this life-transforming knowledge will not be forced upon us. God has done His part.

Yet someone may venture to comment, "I know all about the Bible, and it has not changed any aspect of my life." This testimony could be recited all too often by countless individuals who live a marginalized existence. There is a tremendous difference between knowing the truth and appropriating the truth. When we personally apply God's truth to our souls, we are enabled to live beyond the effects of our sinful selves. However, when knowledge takes residence only in our minds and does not become a motivator for action, God's treasure remains undiscovered.

And we can be sure that we know him if we obey his commandments. If someone claims, "I know God," but doesn't obey God's commandments, that person is a liar and is not living in the truth. But those who obey God's word truly show how completely they love him. That is how we know we are living in him. Those who say they live in God should live their lives as Jesus did.

—1 John 2:3–6

There are two access points from which we may qualify to enter into God's grace. The first is faith, believing what God has said. The second is obedience, doing what God has said. Navigating these pathways will enable the Christian to negotiate all of life's challenges and experience Jesus Christ as relevant to every area of life.

So we have not stopped praying for you since we first heard about you. We ask God to give you complete knowledge of his will and to give you spiritual wisdom and understanding. Then the way you live will always honor and please the Lord, and your lives will produce every kind of good fruit. All the while, you will grow as you learn to know God better and better.

—Col. 1:9–10

A deceptive treasure map leads us to search for a grace that only excuses our wrongdoing rather than enables our right doing. We would rather God overlook our sinfulness than to empower us to live beyond it. While indulging ourselves with the gratifications of the flesh, we claim to be partakers of God's grace. As a result, we miss the true nature of grace as being the power of God unto salvation that delivers us, not just theoretically but authentically, from the dictates of our sinful passions. Content with a theology of tolerance, we prefer not to be transformed. We have lost sight of the fact that God expects us to change by partaking of His grace. "By his divine power, God has given us everything we need for living a godly life" (2 Peter 1:3).

As surrendered followers of Jesus Christ who live in desperate dependency upon Him, we are empowered by God to live beyond ourselves. The power to live Christ's life on earth cannot be manufactured by our own efforts. We are not even capable of conceptualizing the process. Human beings on a quest for their own best interest usually resort toward self-indulgence or self-promotion, thinking self-empowerment is somehow the solution to their powerless condition.

Seeking within our own strength to create our own grace always leads to some form of illicit dependency, addiction; some inappropriate behavior, deviance; some undesirable state of being, mental illness; or some irreversible consequence, death. Thus grace must come *to* us not *through* us. In God's economy we are the recipients of His grace, not the progenitors of it.

Benefactor

As our benefactor, God provides from the resources of His kindness, love, and mercy, through the abundance of His grace, to complete our souls. He does not give us what we deserve, but from an overflow of His generosity. It is ironic that when we think of God's benefits, we most often visualize our version of what the blessing should look like. We often miss experiencing God as our benefactor, because we want Him to bequeath to us people, positions, and possessions, believing that through these we would be fulfilled. Titus 3:4–7 enumerates the blessings bestowed on us by God in the past, as well as those for the present and the future.

> But—"When God our Savior revealed his kindness and love, he saved us, not because of the righteous things we had done, but because of his mercy. He washed away our sins, giving us a new birth and new life through the Holy Spirit. He generously poured out the Spirit upon us through Jesus Christ our Savior. Because of his grace he declared us righteous and gave us confidence that we will inherit eternal life."

The riches of Christ encompass the legacy God bestows on His children.

> But when the right time came, God sent his Son, born of a woman, subject to the law. God sent him to buy freedom for us who were slaves to the law, so that he could adopt us as his very own children. And because we are his children, God has sent the Spirit of his Son into our hearts, prompting us to call out, "Abba, Father." Now you are no longer a slave but God's own child. And since you are his child, God has made you his heir.
> —Gal. 4:4–7

The benefits of God include His purchasing our freedom through His Son, Jesus Christ. This freedom affords the privilege of entering His home as His child, where we can sit at His table dressed in our royal robes washed in the blood of Jesus. The price was not paid to merely release us to seek our independence or to indulge ourselves with the pleasures of this world. We are now free to belong to Him. It is sad, however, when the selfish mind misses this whole truth and insists freedom gives liberty to sin and do what we want to do when we want to do it. For these deluded individuals, eternal life in heaven is more important than being children of God. The idea of a relationship with Jesus holds no value to such people. It is yet another form of indulgence waiting for them in the next life of everlasting bliss. But for the authentic Christian, relationship with Jesus is vital. Possessing the privilege of the position as His child, our persistent pursuit is His divine nature and Christlikeness.

"And because of his glory and excellence, he has given us great and precious promises. These are the promises that enable you to share his divine nature and escape the world's corruption caused by human desires" (2 Peter 1:4).

The great and precious promises of God connect us to His divine nature. As a result of this connection, we possess the moral capacity to be holy and the emotional ability to be healthy. His promises give us the direction to arrive at His ultimate destination of Christlikeness.

> Therefore, dear brothers and sisters, you have no obligation to do what your sinful nature urges you to do. For if you live by its dictates, you will die. But if through the power of the Spirit you put to death the deeds of your sinful nature, you will live. For all who are led by the Spirit of God are children of God.
>
> So you have not received a spirit that makes you fearful slaves. Instead, you received God's Spirit when he adopted you as his own children. Now we call him, "Abba, Father." For his Spirit joins with our spirit to affirm that we are God's children. And since we are his children, we are his heirs. In fact, together with Christ we are heirs of God's glory. But if we are to share his glory, we must also share his suffering.
>
> Yet what we suffer now is nothing compared to the glory he will reveal to us later.
>
> —Rom. 8:12–18

Although we are not fully aware of all aspects of our inheritance, God's promises provide a taste of the expectations He fulfills so we may live with earnest anticipation as we experience His life living through us. His promises are not merely for the hereafter, but encompass life here and now.

God provides the solution for life change. By acting on His promises we have His resolution to all problems and deliverance from the social ills that plague us. We do not comprehend that the solutions to all of life's problems stem from believing and acting on the promises of God. God is literally saying to you, "I can solve your emotional problems, your parenting problems, your relationship problems, your mental problems, all of your problems, if you will trust My truths." If our Christianity does not make a difference with our problems, then we have a problem with our Christianity.

God is extending deliverance to us as we rely on Him. "It is not by force nor by strength, but by my Spirit, says the LORD of Heaven's Armies" (Zech. 4:6). The question is, will you in your desperation depend on God? Will you respond to the invitation God gives to you? Will you continue in your self-effort? Will you believe the same lies? Will you commit the same sins? Will you experience the same problems over and over again? Or will you realize that you are a child of the King with an inheritance already in your possession?

God's job is to bring us into the image of His Son, Jesus Christ, by whatever holy means are appropriate. God uses love to promote purity (1 John 3:1–3), goodness to promote repentance (Rom. 2:4), patience to promote redemption (Luke 8:4–15), discipline to produce maturity (Heb. 12:5–10), and pain to promote growth (Heb. 12:11). God uses trials to bring us to completion (James 1:2–4), tribulation to produce hope (Rom. 5:3–5), trauma of truth to produce brokenness (2 Cor. 7:8–11), and thorns in the flesh to produce dependency (2 Cor. 12:7–10). All His blessings are for achieving the one purpose of transforming us into the image of Jesus Christ. This endeavor is His most important task. All facets of God's economy function to produce Jesus' image within our souls, bringing glory to Him as we depend on Him. God produces His essence within us as we yield to Him.

God has no higher concern and espouses no greater agenda than to promote Jesus as preeminent within our lives. Thus His grace is dedicated to this mission. Grace cannot be manipulated or exploited to achieve our own selfish ambition, nor will it be subservient to our vain conceit. Grace resides securely within the heart and mind of God, having no other master, and can be wielded by none other than His hand.

God initiated His job before the foundation of the world and continues to complete His work. "And I am certain that God, who began the good work within you, will continue his work until it is finally finished on the day when Christ Jesus returns" (Phil. 1:6). Because of all He has done, is doing, and will continue to do, as His creation we should acknowledge His rightful place in our lives. "You are worthy, O Lord our God, / to receive glory and honor and power. / For you created all things, / and they exist because you created what you pleased" (Rev. 4:11).

Unfortunately, when we consider God's job in our lives, we think we are merely saved from hell and destined for heaven. But God has provided so much more for us. The salvation Christ offers is not merely for escape from hell, or membership in heaven. Rather, it is an invitation to a relationship with the living God! Through His great and precious promises He enables us to experience abundant life now and an eternal inheritance beyond comprehension.

That is what the Scriptures mean when they say,

"No eye has seen, no ear has heard,
    and no mind has imagined
what God has prepared
    for those who love him."

But it was to us that God revealed these things by his Spirit. For his Spirit searches out everything and shows us God's deep secrets. No one can know a person's thoughts except that person's own spirit, and no one can know God's thoughts except God's own Spirit. And we have received God's Spirit (not the world's spirit), so we can know the wonderful things God has freely given us.

—1 Cor. 2:9–12

Insight Journal

1. To me it is significant that Jesus is my Savior because:
2. To me it is significant that Jesus is my Sustainer because:
3. To me it is significant that Jesus is my Benefactor because:
4. What do I need from God to get through my day?
5. How should these verses affect the way I live?

> "My thoughts are nothing like your thoughts," says the Lord.
>   "And my ways are far beyond anything you could imagine.
> For just as the heavens are higher than the earth,
>   so my ways are higher than your ways
>   and my thoughts higher than your thoughts."

—Isa. 55:8–9

Psalms Prayer Pattern

Not to us, O LORD, not to us,
　　but to your name goes all the glory
　　for your unfailing love and faithfulness.
Why let the nations say,
　　"Where is their God?"
Our God is in the heavens,
　　and he does as he wishes.
Their idols are merely things of silver and gold,
　　shaped by human hands.
They have mouths but cannot speak,
　　and eyes but cannot see.
They have ears but cannot hear,
　　and noses but cannot smell.
They have hands but cannot feel,
　　and feet but cannot walk,
　　and throats but cannot make a sound.
And those who make idols are just like them,
　　as are all who trust in them.

O Israel, trust the LORD!
　　He is your helper and your shield.
O priests, descendants of Aaron, trust the LORD!
　　He is your helper and your shield.
All you who fear the LORD, trust the LORD!
　　He is your helper and your shield.

The LORD remembers us and will bless us.
　　He will bless the people of Israel
　　and bless the priests, the descendants of Aaron.
He will bless those who fear the LORD,
　　both great and lowly.

May the LORD richly bless
　　both you and your children.
May you be blessed by the LORD,
　　who made heaven and earth.
The heavens belong to the LORD,
　　but he has given the earth to all humanity.
The dead cannot sing praises to the LORD,
　　for they have gone into the silence of the grave.
But we can praise the LORD
　　both now and forever!
Praise the LORD!

　　　　　　　　　　　　　　　　　　　　—Ps. 115

CHAPTER 8

My Way or His Will?

UNFORTUNATELY, ALL TOO often we lose sight of the treasures God has in store for us, and we continue to search for trinkets we perceive to be valuable. While we work against what God wants to do in our lives, we continue to assert our way over His will. Gratefully, God installed a warning system that can be used to determine when things are not going as expected. Anger is evidenced when either God's expectations are being violated or when my personal expectations are being violated.

Some of us grew up in homes where we were taught it is a sin to be angry. With harsh tones we were reprimanded: "Don't you be angry. Don't you know it is a sin to be angry?"

During our first years of marriage I (Melanie) found myself angry frequently. I really did not want to be sinful, but it seemed as though I could not control my anger. Very little was what I expected it to be.

In my desperate search for peace, I decided to take the year to read through my Bible in search of God's perspective on anger. My goal was to read from Genesis to Revelation. Each time I encountered the words *anger*, *angry*, or *wrath* I would circle them. I began circling in Genesis. More references in Exodus and Leviticus. By the time I was in Numbers I realized I had been doing a lot of circling and decided to see what kind of themes were popping up. Who was getting angry? What were they angry about? What happened when they got angry?

To my great surprise I noticed that anger was mentioned most frequently in relation to God! How could this be if it is a sin to be angry? God cannot sin! Apparently I had learned some false theology!

Psalm 4:4 sheds some more light on the topic: "Don't sin by letting anger control you." This passage is reiterated in the New Testament: "In your anger do not sin" (Eph. 4:26 NIV). Verse 27 emphasizes the reason why we should not let anger control us: "for anger gives a foothold to the devil." Since I really do not want the devil to have a foothold in my life, I must be diligently cautious to make sure God is in control of my anger, not I.

It seems apparent that there are times we can be angry and sinful, but there can also be times we can be angry without being sinful. So what is the difference?

Deuteronomy 6:15 states, "The LORD your God, who lives among you, is a jealous God. His anger will flare up against you, and he will wipe you from the face of the earth." But wait a minute! God is jealous, too? I thought that was another character trait that was sinful!

Webster's dictionary defines *jealous* as "intolerant of rivalry or unfaithfulness."[1] God can be jealous because He has no rival! In like fashion, God can be angry and not sinful because He is the only one who has a right to expect anything! Since He is God, He created the world and all that is in it. He established the order of all that is. Therefore, He knows exactly what to expect and has every right to expect things to go according to His blueprint.

Anger is a God-given emotion designed to assist in addressing issues. We get angry as the result of unmet expectations. Something we expected to happen did not occur. Our anger is not sinful when we expect the same things God expects. Sin enters the scenario when we expect our self-centered expectations to be met. As Creator and Sustainer, God is justified in having His expectations met. However, because I am not God, I have no right to demand that my expectations be fulfilled. When we assert that our way must be followed, we are usurping God and elevating ourselves above His position. This idolatry is sin, and the anger that results from expecting to get our own way is also sin.

Once again we see our need to be desperately dependent on God to empower us to live a godly life. Apart from God we have no rights. Apart from His way we can have no peace. In our own strength, life will never be what we want. We are incapable without Him. Therefore with repentant hearts, we must submit ourselves to His plan and allow Him to direct every path. "Trust in the LORD with all your heart, / And lean not on your own understanding; / In all your ways acknowledge Him, / And He shall direct your paths" (Prov. 3:5–6 NKJV).

Too often we are stuck in our anger and ruminate on the offenses until they fester in our souls. As we consider the impact on an individual, we can recognize there is a transgression progression that begins with unmet expectations resulting in frustration, hurt, and anger. A transgression that results in anger may move to resentment and progress to bitterness. Yielding to the temptation, we shift to demanding satisfaction and seeking revenge. Because

ANGER TREE

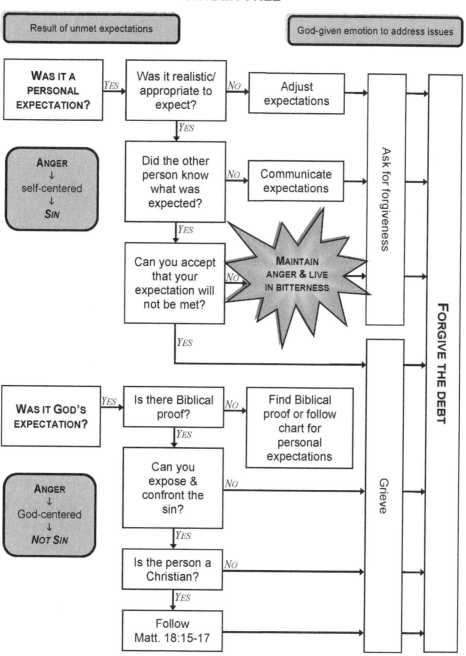

Result of unmet expectations	God-given emotion to address issues

WAS IT A PERSONAL EXPECTATION? — *YES* → Was it realistic/appropriate to expect? — *NO* → Adjust expectations

ANGER ↓ self-centered ↓ **SIN**

Was it realistic/appropriate to expect? — *YES* ↓ Did the other person know what was expected? — *NO* → Communicate expectations

Did the other person know what was expected? — *YES* ↓ Can you accept that your expectation will not be met? — *NO* → MAINTAIN ANGER & LIVE IN BITTERNESS

Can you accept that your expectation will not be met? — *YES* →

Ask for forgiveness

WAS IT GOD'S EXPECTATION? — *YES* → Is there Biblical proof? — *NO* → Find Biblical proof or follow chart for personal expectations

ANGER ↓ God-centered ↓ **NOT SIN**

Is there Biblical proof? — *YES* ↓ Can you expose & confront the sin? — *NO* →

Can you expose & confront the sin? — *YES* ↓ Is the person a Christian? — *NO* →

Is the person a Christian? — *YES* ↓ Follow Matt. 18:15-17 →

Grieve

FORGIVE THE DEBT

"When you are angry, do not sin. Think about these things quietly as you go to bed. Do what is right as a sacrifice to the Lord. And trust the Lord." (Ps. 4:4 ICB)

we cannot achieve satisfaction, the situation may degenerate into hatred. "But anyone who hates another brother or sister is still living and walking in darkness. Such a person does not know the way to go, having been blinded by the darkness" (1 John 2:11).

To avoid being "blinded by the darkness" we can follow a series of determinative questions to clarify how we should proceed. You will notice that all branches on the "Anger Tree" culminate in forgiveness. But it is not necessarily an easy path.

Was It a Personal Expectation?

We have already stated that anger is a God-given emotion to address unmet expectations. When anger begins to arise we must ask, "What did I expect?" Often just identifying our expectations can assist in determining how to proceed.

Was it a personal expectation, or was it God's expectation? Most of the time, we must admit that personal expectations arouse our anger. We wanted our way, and events did not occur as we expected. Our self-centered sense of entitlement convinces us we must have everything we want.

Then we must ask, "Was it realistic and appropriate to expect?" Suppose you determine you expected your newborn baby to never cry. Is that realistic and appropriate to expect? Of course not! Perhaps you expect your spouse to be able to read your mind. Is that realistic and appropriate to expect? No.

When we conclude that our expectation has not been realistic or appropriate, then we must adjust our expectations. I must expect my newborn baby will cry when it is hungry, wet, afraid, or just plain needy. I must expect that my spouse is not omniscient and requires communication before he can understand me.

With the realization that I have fallen short in my expectations, I must ask for forgiveness and forgive the debt. As a result of believing someone has not measured up to our expectations, we are convinced that they owe us something. Remember, this is where our anger can become sinful, because God is the only one who has a right to anything. They do not owe us; they owe God. If we are merely expecting to have our selfish ambitions satisfied, we are sinful. With repentant hearts we must say, "I am sorry I expected you to _____. Will you please forgive me for being unrealistic and inappropriate in my expectation?" If the anger has been aroused without the knowledge of the offending party, this may only need to be a prayer uttered to God, yielding all our desires to Him.

Suppose we did have a realistic and appropriate expectation. "Did the other person know what was expected?" If I expect each family member to take his or her plate from the table at the end of the meal, I must communicate that expectation. If I never convey my expectation and my anger flares because someone left a dinner plate on the table, I must ask for forgiveness and forgive their offense. Truthfully, women can be the worst at expecting things they have not communicated. "Why in the world did he get me a blender for our twenty-fifth wedding anniversary? He should have known I wanted a new ring!"

If you have determined that your personal expectation was realistic and appropriate, and the other person knew what was expected, you are faced with the next question: "Can I accept that my expectation will not be met?" Since you are not God, you do not have a right to have all your expectations met. Can you accept that? Unfortunately, this is the point where we often get stuck. We maintain our anger and live in bitterness for hours, days, months, and even years because our expectation was not realized. The only recourse to resolve the anger and bitterness is to ask for forgiveness and forgive the debt. Although we repeatedly come to the point of asking for forgiveness and forgiving the debt in this flow chart, I am in no way suggesting that is always easy. We will be addressing the complex subject of forgiveness in a later chapter.

Grief

Perhaps you *must* accept that your expectation will not be met. Grief may result. Grieving is the process of adjusting your life because something is lost. Imagine that your best friend's dog just had puppies, and you were promised the cutest puppy in the litter. As you waited for the puppy to be old enough to leave its mother, you prepared a doghouse, purchased bowls for water and food, chose the perfect nourishment, and even bought a few toys. As you awaited the arrival of your newest family member, you studied the training manuals and decided where you would go for obedience school. With eager anticipation you drove to pick up *your* puppy, only to be disappointed by the fact that *your* puppy had been given to someone else! What a loss! You could maintain your anger and live in bitterness, but you still have to adjust your life to the fact that you will not have the cutest puppy from the litter. Sure, there are a lot of options, and as you decide between those options you are adjusting to the loss—grieving.

For an illustration on the lighter side concerning grieving, consider a woman with a closet full of shoe racks. All her shoes are organized as beautifully as a rainbow. While she was running around in attempts to maintain her hectic schedule, a heel broke off one of her shoes and a strap malfunctioned on another pair. A closer inspection revealed several other pairs of shoes in disrepair. As she removed the imperfect shoes from her racks, she was faced with empty spaces—loss. Being a perfectionist with obsessive-compulsive features, she reorganized her life and her shoe racks based on the loss. After a shopping adventure she filled some spaces with new shoes, and other shoes moved to fill in the empty gaps. Instead of sorrowing with no hope about the ruined shoes, she reorganized her closet and her life based on the truth that she could adjust her life in spite of the loss.

As we adjust and reorganize our lives based on a loss, there are two avenues we may take. We may fall into toxic grief, or we may choose healthy grief.

Toxic grief results when we adjust our lives based on lies. Our choices are poisoned by the deception we accept as truth. The downward spiral of toxic grief may resemble this scenario: "I lost my job; I have no way to support my family; I am worthless; we won't have any food; our house will go into foreclosure; we will be on the streets at Christmastime; my life is over."

Healthy grief views loss from the perspective of God's truths. The same scenario can result in praise and earnest expectation: "I lost my job because I stood for what is right; God promises He will supply my every need (Phil. 4:19); God declares He will never leave me or forsake me (Heb. 13:5); He knows the plans He has for me (Jer. 29:11); I can trust God (Ps. 28:7)."

Grief issues span the spectrum of what might be considered insignificant to some through extreme crisis situations. It is the essence of grief to coexist with what we cannot control, and it is essential that we are content in Christ while coexisting with what we can't control. The intensity of the grief often reveals the value an individual has placed on a person, position, or possession. In the resolution of grief it is imperative to recognize Christ as relevant to every situation we encounter. "How does God expect me to adjust my life based on this loss and remembering His love, care, and trustworthiness?" Yes, this applies to puppies, shoes, cancer, divorce, death, and every other scenario we can conjure up. God is fully capable of handling us through everything!

Was It God's Expectation?

If we suspect that an unmet expectation has resulted in anger concerning an issue that God would also be angry about, we must first ask, "Is there biblical proof?" Many times we assume God would be angry about a particular situation, but we cannot find the scriptural backing for our assertion. So often we seek for biblical proof to justify our own solution to accomplish the end result we desire. We must truly seek His solutions. Seeking Him in desperate dependency will unveil His plan. But if we cannot find biblical proof, then we are obliged to follow the Anger Tree regarding a personal expectation.

With biblical proof evident, our next decision to consider is this: "Can I expose and confront the sin?" We can never be ready to confront what is in others' lives until we are content in Christ with the way things are in our lives. Otherwise we may be trying to control people and situations to make *our* lives better instead of ministering Christ to others. Although we are admonished to expose and confront sin, there may be extenuating circumstances that may prevent such an action. Perhaps the offending party has already died, and we are unable to confront the sin. The resulting grief would address the truth that God is the ultimate judge who will see that justice is meted out. Our part is to allow God to handle the situation and forgive the debt.

"Is the person a Christian?" This criterion does make a difference because God offers a specific course of action for guilty Christians. If the wrongdoer is not a Christian, we must grieve and allow God to mete out His justice as we forgive the debt. Remember, grieving is about adjusting our lives based on the truth. In regard to the unsaved, we must realize the truth that unsaved individuals are unable to conduct themselves with the love, grace, and mercy of a forgiven soul. They cannot be held to the same standards God expects of the saved. Often we jump to confrontation and boundary setting without grieving the truth that a person cannot evidence godliness and goodness apart from the grace of Christ. Rather than being angry with the sinner, we must grieve for his or her soul. "It isn't my responsibility to judge outsiders, but it certainly is your responsibility to judge those inside the church who are sinning. God will judge those on the outside; but as the Scriptures say, 'You must remove the evil person from among you'" (1 Cor. 5:12–13).

If the offending party is a Christian, Matthew 18:15–17 provides guidelines on how to address the situation.

> If another believer sins against you, go privately and point out the offense. If the other person listens and confesses it, you have won that person back. But if you are unsuccessful, take one or two others with you and go back again, so that everything you say may be confirmed by two or three witnesses. If the person still refuses to listen, take your case

to the church. Then if he or she won't accept the church's decision, treat that person as a pagan or a corrupt tax collector.

Many people are surprised to learn that Jesus taught there are times we are to "treat that person as a pagan or a corrupt tax collector." In those days, if a corrupt tax collector saw you on the street and said you owed $10,000 in taxes, you would be required to pay or you would be put in jail. So the corrupt tax collectors were avoided with extreme measures. It would not be uncommon for people to walk on the other side of the street with eyes down in order to circumvent any contact. Can you believe Jesus would actually promote such conduct? Yes, there are actually times when we should make wide circles to steer clear of people.

But as we are addressing these situations that cause anger to us and to God, we ultimately must grieve the truth and forgive the debt. God is the final authority, and it is His job to see that the appropriate judgment is satisfied. We must yield to His way and give up our will in all areas of our lives.

As I was fine-tuning the Anger Tree, I was presented with a test. Kirk and I were preparing to celebrate our tenth wedding anniversary. Too many times I had experienced anger because I was unrealistic and inappropriate, and because I did not communicate my expectations. I determined to work to avoid that anger on our anniversary. With our anniversary on June 8, I routinely began communicating my expectations in January.

"For our tenth anniversary I would really like to have a ring," I said.

As a matter of background, you should understand that we had two young girls at the time, and I was a stay-at-home mom. Finances were tight, so jewelry was not a typical request for me. I was giving him plenty of notice.

"For our tenth anniversary I would really like to have a ring," I repeated in February.

Kirk acknowledged hearing the request.

So he would have plenty of time to save and shop, I repeated my request again in March. "For our tenth anniversary I would really like to have a ring."

I really didn't change the wording much each time I let my expectations be known, because I wanted to be sure there was clarity in the expectation. But in April the wording changed a little. "I would really like to have a ring for our tenth anniversary."

Perhaps you noticed that I did not request a carat diamond ring. Not even a diamond ring! I was being a little elementary about it and just wanted a ring to show off to my friends. I had anticipated going to church on Sunday and shaking my hand in the faces of my friends as I squealed, "Look what my husband gave me for our tenth anniversary!"

We had some very difficult years preceding our tenth anniversary, and I was hoping for something concrete to verify that those years were behind us. So in May I reiterated my request: "You do remember that I said I would really like a ring for our tenth anniversary, right?" An affirmative response followed.

On the morning of June 8, I awoke with eager anticipation. I could hardly wait to see the ring Kirk had picked out for me! He had invited me to a fancy restaurant for the evening, and arrangements had been made for the girls. As I dressed in my festive attire, the expectant grin would not come off my face.

In the form of a perfect gentleman, Kirk ushered me to our romantic setting as I prepared to be wowed. After we placed our orders, Kirk jubilantly proclaimed, "I have a present for you."

"Really?" I teased.

With an expansive grin on his face, he slowly reached into his jacket pocket and presented me with a velvet jewelry box. I tried not to let my smile fall, but my heart sank. This was not a ring box! It was too big for a ring box! *Okay, let's not lose hope yet; maybe there is more in the box than just a ring.* "Go ahead, open it."

I reluctantly complied.

Inside the blue velvet box was the most beautiful…dainty…delicate…opal *necklace!* I was speechless.

Kirk began expounding on the intricacies of the opal. I was speechless as I stared at the necklace.

Next he tried to educate me on the coloring of opals. I was still speechless.

He proceeded to point out the details of the gold filigree surrounding the opal. I was still speechless.

As he elaborated on the delicate chain, my brain started screaming, *I have two little girls who will have this ripped off my neck before I make it through the door!* But I remained speechless.

By then Kirk must have noticed my silence, because he asked, "Don't you like it?"

"It's pretty," was my reply.

With more conviction he asked again, "Don't you like it?"

"It's pretty," I repeated.

With another sales pitch regarding all the beauty of the necklace he asked again, "Don't you like it?"

Can I accept that my expectation will not be met? was the question that echoed in my mind. I was faced with maintaining anger and living in bitterness. Too many years had already passed where we were stuck in that place. I really didn't want to go there again.

I finally said, "I asked for a ring."

"Yes, but don't you like it?"

I reiterated one more time, "I asked for a ring."

"Well, if you really don't like it, we can take it back and get you a ring."

"Okay." With a grateful heart, I closed the lid on the necklace and made plans to shop for my ring as soon as dinner was finished. Before the evening was over we had purchased a beautiful, delicate, dainty, opal ring!

I think it is pretty easy to see that scenario conveys a personal expectation. I certainly could not find biblical proof that God would have been angry if I did not get a ring for our tenth anniversary. Was it realistic and appropriate to expect? In Kirk's defense, he still contends that he did not think we could afford a ring. I still assert that he would have done better to get a ring out of the gumball machine than to buy me a necklace! Did the other person know what was expected? Hmm…Let me think here…I certainly communicated my expectations! So there I sat, confronted with the question "Can you accept that your expectation will not be met?" I knew the choice I faced either led to maintaining anger and living in bitterness, or grieving. I really did not like either of the options. As I worked to trust the Lord, He jubilantly made another way of escape! Yay, God! And thank you, Kirk.

The International Children's Bible translates Psalm 4:4–5, "When you are angry, do not sin. Think about these things quietly as you go to bed. Do what is right as a sacrifice to the Lord. And trust the Lord." Too often I find it is not easy to think about the things I am angry about quietly as I go to bed. In my muttering and sputtering I am reminded that I must do what is right. Doing what is right requires me to offer up everything to the Lord as a sacrifice. It cannot be mine any longer. I must give all my rights and expectations to Him. How in the world can I do that? I must trust the Lord. At the end of the day, all outcomes are His responsibility. Can I trust Him? Will you trust Him?

Insight Journal

For this Insight Journal, prayerfully consider at least five situations when you became angry. Consider each situation separately and follow the Anger Tree while answering these questions:

- I got angry when I expected (describe the situation):
- Was it a personal expectation or God's expectation?
- Was it realistic and appropriate to expect?
- Did the other person know what was expected?
- What do I need to apologize for?
- Can I accept that my expectation will not be met?
- Is there biblical proof that this is God's expectation? Where?
- How does God expect me to proceed?
- What do I need to forgive?

Psalms Prayer Pattern

I will exalt you, my God and King,
    and praise your name forever and ever.
I will praise you every day;
    yes, I will praise you forever.
Great is the LORD! He is most worthy of praise!
    No one can measure his greatness.

Let each generation tell its children of your mighty acts;
    let them proclaim your power.
I will meditate on your majestic, glorious splendor
    and your wonderful miracles.
Your awe-inspiring deeds will be on every tongue;
    I will proclaim your greatness.
Everyone will share the story of your wonderful goodness;
    they will sing with joy about your righteousness.

The LORD is merciful and compassionate,
    slow to get angry and filled with unfailing love.
The LORD is good to everyone.
    He showers compassion on all his creation.
All of your works will thank you, LORD,
    and your faithful followers will praise you.
They will speak of the glory of your kingdom;
    they will give examples of your power.
They will tell about your mighty deeds
    and about the majesty and glory of your reign.
For your kingdom is an everlasting kingdom.
    You rule throughout all generations.

The LORD always keeps his promises;
   he is gracious in all he does.
The LORD helps the fallen
   and lifts those bent beneath their loads.
The eyes of all look to you in hope;
   you give them their food as they need it.
When you open your hand,
   you satisfy the hunger and thirst of every living thing.
The LORD is righteous in everything he does;
   he is filled with kindness.
The LORD is close to all who call on him,
   yes, to all who call on him in truth.
He grants the desires of those who fear him;
   he hears their cries for help and rescues them.
The LORD protects all those who love him,
   but he destroys the wicked.

I will praise the LORD,
   and may everyone on earth bless his holy name
   forever and ever.

—Ps. 145

CHAPTER 9

Resigning the God Job

I T IS A tremendous delight to watch children "play house." A toddler may make the announcement that she will fix dinner for the family and then proceed to her play kitchen. Pulling a pot from the cabinet she lists the ingredients that will be included: ketchup, macaroni, carrots, cereal, cheese, but no peas! In the mixing bowl she plans to add salad, mustard, salt, and hamburgers, of course. But wait! She still has to fix the chicken nuggets! Since the dipping sauce is missing, she broadcasts that she is going to town as she heads out the door with her purse and Mom's car keys. Mom has been chuckling while watching the preparations, but when the toddler actually opens the door to the family car and inserts the keys into the ignition, terror grips her heart. Making a mad dash to rescue her child from "play," Mom reminds the toddler that she is not big enough to drive the car. Of course, a temper tantrum ensues because the toddler has big dinner plans that cannot happen if she does not drive to the store to get dipping sauce for the nuggets! Although Mom may offer alternatives, the toddler will insist, "I want to do it myself!" But the wise mother knows her child is not capable of handling everything she desires.

As children "play house," in our feeble attempts we "play God." We imagine a multitude of strategies to promote our self-interest in order to feel good about ourselves and avoid pain. Usually we are controlling every situation perceivable. During our playtime we may say things such as, "Show me how to control my situation better"; "Give me more ideas on how to please myself"; "Teach me to be a better god." We stomp our feet and assert, "I want to do it myself without any help!" Our self-sufficient attitude exudes extreme confidence in our own ability and worth. But an all-wise God knows we are not capable of handling everything we desire.

An exhausted and exasperated client proclaimed, "I just wish the world would stop so I could take some time off." She was fully convinced that life could not go on without her in control. How many times do we believe it is our sole responsibility to keep everything running decently and in order? In our arrogance we have bought into the lie that anything that is to be done must be done by us. Others are either irresponsible or incapable, and it is our responsibility to maintain balance. Not only do we need to maintain balance, but we must also keep the peace and make sure our family looks normal and happy.

We perceive that our job description includes the responsibilities of savior, sustainer, and benefactor—but this is God's job description and we are not capable of handling His job. When others do not fall in line and follow our leadership so we can be their savior, sustainer, and benefactor, we become angry and bitter. With a long list of debts, we attempt to collect on what we believe is owed to us because we have done such an excellent job at ordering our world.

"You Owe Me"

Idolatry is not just an Old Testament sin. Idolatry is evident in modern times, even in America, when we assert control and expect others to acknowledge our authority. Usurping God's authority results in the violation of the first commandment, which states, "You must not have any other god but me" (Deut. 5:7). We insist on being idolized when we put ourselves in the place of authority as we attempt to control others and ourselves. Even when we demand that someone "owes" us, we are placing ourselves in the position of a god who maintains that justice is our responsibility.

True forgiveness evidences a relationship that is desperately dependent on God as we let go of our desires to control and give up our rights to seek satisfaction by our own means. As we forgive, we are demonstrating that Christ is trustworthy and that we can rely on Him to resolve our crisis as we relinquish to Him those who have wronged us. When others do not measure up to our expectations, we must realize that it is not our expectations they must live up to, but God's. As a result, we venture to release our expectations to God's guidance, allowing Him to be responsible for our lives and to be evident as our Savior, sustainer, and benefactor.

It is vitally important to realize that only God can forgive sins. The forgiveness we are commanded to give is for our benefit, that we may depend upon Him and walk rightly with Him. "And be ye kind one to another, tenderhearted, forgiving one another, even as God for Christ's sake hath forgiven you" (Eph. 4:32 KJV). We are releasing the offending party from our condemnation, and we are removing ourselves from the burden of seeking satisfaction. In actuality, the forgiveness we are to offer should assert, "You don't owe me anything." Our job is to take ourselves out of the role of playing God, and allow God to be responsible to see that justice is administered. The all-powerful God will lift the weight of our anger and bitterness when we forgive in a manner that passes the responsibility for retribution to the only One who is capable of righteously administering justice.

Often when Jesus taught about forgiveness He used a financial illustration to convey the concept. Therefore, as I (Melanie) attempted to grasp the practical application of forgiveness, I considered our office policies regarding finances. Before our counseling office turned the corner to the technological computer age, client accounts were maintained on ledger cards similar to this:

LEDGER
Statement of Account

Date	Description	Charge	Payment	Adjust	Balance

To understand how these cards were utilized, let's consider a scenario. A woman in her early fifties, we'll call Mindy, came for counseling regarding her troubled marriage. She told of her disinterested husband who seemed to be absorbed in a multiplicity of diversions that excluded her. During Mindy's initial session she conveyed her heartache and feelings of rejection. Quite obviously this situation could not be resolved in one session, so we made plans to continue at a future date.

As Mindy left the office, the receptionist entered the following information on her ledger card:

Date	Description	Charge	Payment	Adjust	Balance
02/20/02	initial session	60.00			60.00
02/20/02	check		60.00		-0-

Subsequent sessions unveiled more of Mindy's story. She had found her husband's stash of pornographic magazines that led her to check his web site history. When she learned that he had given himself to lustful desires, she wondered how far those lustful desires had taken him. His cell phone history revealed the shocking truth that another woman had become the object of his affections.

Each time Mindy left the office, the receptionist documented her visits on her ledger card:

Date	Description	Charge	Payment	Adjust	Balance
02/20/02	initial session	60.00			60.00
02/20/02	check		60.00		-0-
02/27/02	2nd session	60.00			60.00
02/27/02	check		60.00		-0-
03/06/02	3rd session	60.00			60.00
03/06/02	check		60.00		-0-
03/13/02	4th session (forgot checkbook)	60.00			60.00
03/20/02	5th session	60.00			120.00
03/20/02	check		120.00		-0-

The devastation that resulted from her husband's unfaithfulness prompted insecurity and anxiety. Along with the couple's angry outbursts and malicious threats, the instability of the marriage reflected in the finances. Her husband had left the home, and uncertainty gripped Mindy's future. With fearful tears she asked if there was any possibility of assistance to pay for her counseling.

A sketchy financial disclosure indicated the need for relief, so the office granted a courtesy discount. This courtesy discount allowed Mindy to pay $30 for each session and be relieved of the remaining balance. Her ledger card reflected the arrangement.

Date	Description	Charge	Payment	Adjust	Balance
03/27/02	6th session	60.00			60.00
03/27/02	check		30.00		30.00
03/27/02	courtesy discount			30.00	-0-

During the seventh session Mindy announced that her husband had filed for divorce. He had not been providing her with any financial support, but she felt confident that when the divorce was finalized she would receive a large settlement. The succeeding sessions remained unpaid, but the office continued to offer the courtesy discount.

Date	Description	Charge	Payment	Adjust	Balance
04/03/02	7th session	60.00			60.00
04/03/02	courtesy discount			30.00	30.00
04/10/02	8th session	60.00			90.00
04/10/02	courtesy discount			30.00	60.00
04/17/02	9th session	60.00			120.00
04/17/02	courtesy discount			30.00	90.00

Spring fever must have hit, because Mindy did not come back for counseling. Billing statements were sent to remind her of the unpaid balance. Thirty days past due. Sixty days past due. Ninety days past due, but no communication from Mindy.

The office began making phone calls in attempts to collect the outstanding balance. Messages were left on the answering machine. A phone call to Mindy's workplace revealed that she resigned her position when her divorce was final. Surprisingly, Mindy answered her cell phone.

The office manager politely informed Mindy that her $90 balance was overdue and needed to be paid. With indignant arrogance Mindy protested, "Counseling never helped me one single bit. Now that my divorce is final, I realize that all I needed to do was to be rid of that jerk a long time ago. It wasn't the counseling that helped me get on with my life, so I'm not paying for it."

Complications arise when bad debts remain on the books, so accountants insist that accounts must be settled appropriately. Mindy was sent a notice indicating that her account would be turned over for collection if the debt was not satisfied within ten days. The office was not surprised that no response came, and followed through with the procedure. Mindy's ledger card reflected the action taken.

Date	Description	Charge	Payment	Adjust	Balance
08/15/02	***** to Collection Agency *****			90.00	-0-

After an account is turned over for collection, billing statements cease, phone calls stop, and all activity to collect the outstanding debt is discontinued on the part of the office. However, the collection agency initiates their own set of procedures and penalties and assumes responsibility to see to it that the balance is paid. Interest, fees, and court costs increase the indebtedness as the collection agency continues to accrue the balance.

Eyebrows rose when a frantic call came to the office from Mindy. "I feel like I am going crazy. I really need some help. My kids are all angry with me because they believe I squandered the money I got in the divorce settlement. They think part of it should have been theirs. I don't know what to do. Can you please help me?"

When an account was turned over for collection, various means were employed to flag the default to prevent future failure to pay. With notations like ***!!!Mindy!!!*** the office personnel realized special considerations were necessary. Mindy was reminded of her unpaid balance and told that she could not reschedule until that account was satisfied. With a tearful, cracking voice she insisted, "I'll come right over and take care of that." But the office stated, "You don't owe that balance to us, you owe that to the collection agency. You must settle your account with them, and they will notify us when it has been paid. At that point we will reschedule with you."

Within a short time the collection agency called the office with word that Mindy's account was paid in full. As the appointment was scheduled, Mindy was informed, "You must bring cash with you to pay $60 in full before the session begins." There would be no leeway allowed for a forgotten checkbook, bad checks, credit cards over the limit, or any other diversions. And the courtesy discount was no longer in effect. Mindy's ledger card now included "Cash Basis Only."

Webster's dictionary defines *forgive* as "to give up resentment of or claim to requital for; to grant relief from payment of; to cease to feel resentment against (an offender)."[1] Other definitions include, "refuse to hold an offense against, release from the penalty owed, to cancel the debt." If we combine the definition of forgiveness with the previous financial scenario, we may glean a better understanding of the process of forgiveness.

Somewhere in the past, an individual offended you. We'll call this person Sam. Sam asked for forgiveness after the offense, and you readily accepted his apology.

Date	Description	Charge	Payment	Adjust	Balance
past	offense	+			+
	asked for forgiveness		-		-0-

Not too long after, Sam repeated the offense with a different twist. This second violation incurred a greater charge because you operated under the assumption that Sam was truly repentant and the offense would not happen again. Not only had he offended you, but other sinful characteristics were becoming evident. However, realizing his error, Sam repented again, and you forgave him again.

Date	Description	Charge	Payment	Adjust	Balance
later	offense (charge greater)	+ +			+ +
	asked for forgiveness		- -		-0-

Jesus' disciples must have encountered similar infractions, because Peter asked Jesus, "'Lord, how often should I forgive someone who sins against me? Seven times?'

"'No, not seven times,' Jesus replied, 'but seventy times seven!'" (Matt. 18:21–22).

Certainly there are some people you would like to keep a tally sheet on and mark each time you must forgive, so that when the 490 mark is reached you can finally say, "Your 490 times are up. I'm not forgiving you any more!" But hopefully God is not keeping the same tally sheet for you!

There are also times when a great transgression has occurred, but no apologies are offered. From a graceful heart you may grant relief from the payment of that debt.

Date	Description	Charge	Payment	Adjust	Balance
recently	offense (charge greater)	+ + +			+ + +
	gave forgiveness—not asked for			- - -	-0-

But there may be times when a continued offense cannot be overlooked. Is there any way this debt can be satisfied? Sometimes we may state, "I just want him to say he's sorry." A flippant "I'm sorry" may not measure up to the terms you were expecting to receive. So carefully consider, what will really be enough to satisfy this debt? Terms can be arranged on outstanding accounts while payments are made and trust is regained.

Turned Over for Collection

However, there are also occasions when there is no way a debt can be satisfied because the offense is so great. As with businesses, complications arise when bad debts remain in our lives, so accounts must be settled appropriately. In those times it is essential to turn the account over to our divine collection agency. We must determine that we will no longer exert any energy in the collection of the debt, but allow God to be responsible for the account. With open hands we can release the strongholds that have bound us to our anger and bitterness. The only One who is truly capable of collecting the debt will see to it that justice is served.

Often we are reluctant to allow God to handle our accounts because we are not convinced we will be satisfied with the outcome. How will God settle the account? There are two methods God will use to reconcile outstanding debts. Either the offender will pay in hell for all eternity, or Christ's death will cover the penalty.

"He canceled the record of the charges against us and took it away by nailing it to the cross" (Col. 2:14).

"But if we confess our sins to him, he is faithful and just to forgive us our sins and to cleanse us from all wickedness" (1 John 1:9).

Date	Description	Charge	Payment	Adjust	Balance
today	** to Divine Collection Agency **			- - - -	-0-
	option one		Hell		eternity
	option two		Christ's	Death	-0-

"That's too easy," you may whine. Really? You believe Christ's payment for your sin was too easy? Remember Ephesians 4:32: "Be ye kind one to another, tenderhearted, forgiving one another, *even as God for Christ's sake hath forgiven you*" (emphasis added). In the same way you have been forgiven of your outstanding debts that cannot be satisfied except through Christ's death, He also stands ready to forgive all who come to Him for forgiveness. We are much more eager to accept this forgiveness for ourselves than we are to allow the same justice to be meted out on those who have offended us.

Millions of people have repeated the Lord's Prayer, which states, "and forgive us our sins, as we have forgiven those who sin against us" (Matt. 6:12). Since we only mechanically quote the passage, we neglect to recognize the conditions and terms of forgiveness. Do we really want God to forgive us in the same way we are forgiving others? In the verses immediately following the Lord's Prayer Jesus elaborates further. "If you forgive those who sin against you, your heavenly Father will forgive you. But if you refuse to forgive others, your Father will not forgive your sins" (Matt. 6:14–15). Forgiveness is the evidence of a redeemed soul. Without forgiveness there is no redemption.

Ultimately all sin is an offense against God. "Against you, and you alone, have I sinned; / I have done what is evil in your sight" (Ps. 51:4). Therefore, the debt that is owed as the result of an injustice is ultimately owed to Him. As we lead desperately dependent lives we will allow all debts to be His responsibility. Only God is capable of resolving our crisis. "My soul waits in silence for God only; / From Him is my salvation. / He only is my rock and my salvation, / My stronghold; I shall not be greatly shaken" (Ps. 62:1–2 NASB). "Let all that I am wait quietly before God, / for my hope is in him. / He alone is my rock and my salvation, / my fortress where I will not be shaken. / My victory and honor come from God alone. / He is my refuge, a rock where no enemy can reach me" (Ps. 62:5–7). "Only fear the LORD and serve Him in truth with all your heart; for consider what great things He has done for you" (1 Sam. 12:24 NASB).

So what are you to do after an account has been turned over for collection? It would be wise to make notations ***!!!!!!*** and to be alert for future infractions. Although your personal ledger sheet may indicate a zero balance, when an account is turned over for collection, it has not been settled. You may not forget that the injustice occurred, but you must remember that it is not your duty to see that it is paid. Retribution is not your responsibility. You can be free from the burdens of anger and bitterness while still exercising caution to avoid future violations. "O my people, trust in him at all times. / Pour out your heart to him, / for God is our refuge" (Ps. 62:8). Operate on a "cash basis only" policy as you consider whether trust can be regained. Even though an individual may claim God has forgiven him or her, you must be desperately dependent on His direction for verification of the truth.

Not My Responsibility

Guaranteed, Satan will be tempting you frequently to reclaim the outstanding balance. He will suggest a multitude of methods that you could employ to reassume control and attempt to make sure that the offending party pays for what he or she has done to you. In those moments, you remind Satan and yourself that you are no longer responsible for collecting this debt. You have turned the responsibility over to God, who will handle the account as He sees fit.

Sometimes wounded souls fall for the lie that they must pay for an offense that was done against them. For example, an adolescent may believe she must always carry the shame that was forced on her when she was molested. Or a divorced spouse may never again be happy as a result of the unfaithfulness of his partner. Or a sibling must continuously make allowances and excuses to cover up the deviance of her brother. Do not forget that Satan is the master deceiver, and he is eager to use any device to keep us from experiencing our freedom in Christ.

Here is a lighthearted assessment tool to determine how likely you are to pay for a debt you did not incur. Suppose I (Melanie) find out you have a stash of photographs underneath your bed encompassing generations of family history. It would then become my mission to right this major injustice that has occurred against your family photographs. Together we walk the aisles of a department store where I fill the cart with all the necessary supplies to begin embarking on the adventure of scrapbooking your heritage. A scrapbook, some card stock, journaling pens, adhesive, photo corners, and more accumulate quickly. When we arrive at the register the clerk proclaims, "That will be $63.94." What will you do?

You may look at me, and I will look at you. And you will look at me, and I will say, "She said that will be $63.94." You might become a little agitated at that point and wonder why I am reminding you of the price when I was the one who piled all the stuff in the cart in the first place. After all, you never wanted the stuff to begin with! But too many people get stuck holding the receipt for something they never asked for or wanted, instead of saying, "That is not my debt. I am not paying for it."

By myself I cannot withstand the onslaught of Satan, who unrelentingly attempts to persuade me that I can be solely responsible for all areas of my life. Too many times I have fallen for the lie that I am capable of fulfilling God's job description of Savior, sustainer, and benefactor. But I am not designed to fulfill His job description any more than a two-year-old who is playing house can assume the responsibilities of a wife and mother. Satan makes it look so easy to perform God's responsibilities, while at the same time convincing us that it is so hard to let God be in control!

We must resign from our job of playing God and allow Him to assume His rightful position. He is the only one who can forgive sin, and I must resign from my self-appointed duty of attempting to collect all the debt I believe is owed to me. Because He forgave all my sin, I must continue relying on Him to exercise His righteous justice on my behalf. Not only must I trust Him to forgive my sin, I must rely on Him to redeem me from the sins of others who have hurt me. Without the Holy Spirit's work in our lives, we are totally incapable of living the abundant life He designed for us to experience as a result of our desperately dependent relationship with Him. As we rely on Him to complete His work in our lives, we can experience all He has to offer those who allow Him to reign supreme. "So now, come back to your God. / Act with love and justice, / and always depend on him" (Hos. 12:6).

Insight Journal

Consider at least five accounts that remain open with outstanding balances in your life. For each account, complete a ledger sheet that indicates the charges and the balance due. What attempts have been made to satisfy the outstanding balance? Determine what you will do with each unsettled account. Will you continue to seek satisfaction through your own means? Or will you allow the divine collection agency, God, to be responsible for collecting the debt?

Psalms Prayer Pattern

I cry out to the Lord;
 I plead for the Lord's mercy.
I pour out my complaints before him
 and tell him all my troubles.
When I am overwhelmed,
 you alone know the way I should turn.
Wherever I go,
 my enemies have set traps for me.
I look for someone to come and help me,
 but no one gives me a passing thought!
No one will help me;
 no one cares a bit what happens to me.
Then I pray to you, O Lord.
 I say, "You are my place of refuge.
 You are all I really want in life.
Hear my cry,
 for I am very low.
Rescue me from my persecutors,
 for they are too strong for me.
Bring me out of prison
 so I can thank you.
The godly will crowd around me,
 for you are good to me."

—Ps. 142

PART 3

The Application—Christ Is Enough

CHAPTER 10

What Is My Job?

A RE YOU CONFUSED at this point? Perhaps you have been inundated with all the lists that you need to check off in order to be a good Christian. You want to do right, but you don't know how. If we allow God to be in control of our lives, what is our job?

Bottom line? It is our job to be in a relationship with Jesus Christ. Sorry, but I can't give you a checklist on that one, any more than I can give you a checklist that verifies that you are doing a good job as a husband or a wife. Sure, we may have expectations for our relationship with our spouse like, "Tell me you love me at least once a day"; "Take out the trash"; "Have dinner on the table at 6:00"; "Bring home a paycheck that will pay the bills"; and so forth. But if your spouse could place a checkmark by each of those tasks, does that guarantee a close relationship?

In Mark 12 the Sadducees and Pharisees were debating about all the rules, regulations, and requirements of the law. There were 613 commands in the Torah (Genesis–Deuteronomy). One of the teachers of the law asked Jesus, "Of all the commandments, which is the most important?" (12:28). Restated, "Can You please explain what we're supposed to be doing?"

Jesus answered, "The most important command is this: 'Listen, people of Israel! The Lord our God, he is the only Lord. Love the Lord your God. Love him with all you heart, all your soul, all your mind, and all your strength.' The second most important command is this: 'Love your neighbor as you love yourself.' These two commands are the most important commands."

—Mark 12:29–31 ICB

The Greek word *agapao* translated "love" in these verses means "to welcome, to entertain, to be fond of, to love dearly."[1] Interestingly, this is the same word used in Ephesians 5:25 (KJV, emphasis added): "husbands *love* your wives."

Magnify

Paul describes our job from another perspective: "Therefore, whether you eat or drink, or whatever you do, do all to the glory of God" (1 Cor. 10:31 NKJV). Personally, I (Melanie) had a difficult time with that verse. That all sounds well and good, but how do you "do all to the glory of God"? So I considered Psalm 34:3 (NKJV) for another point of view: "Oh, magnify the LORD with me, and let us exalt His name together."

Suppose I were to hand you a magnifying glass and ask you to describe it. What would you say? After you put it up to your eye and moved it in and out a few times, your first response may be, "It makes things bigger." If I challenged you to keep going with your description, you might add statements such as these:

- It helps you to see better.
- Things are easier to see.
- You can see more details.
- It makes things appear closer.
- You can see things you never saw before.

In science class we were introduced to a microscope, which is also used to magnify. During lab time a few glass slides were offered for investigation. With amazement we examined cells, hair, tadpoles, and a myriad of other items. The classroom filled with exclamations of "Wow!" "Cool!" "You gotta come see this!" "I never knew that was there!" The inquisitive would examine one item after another with astonishment and awe.

When we follow the exhortation given in Psalm 34:3 to "magnify the LORD," we function as a magnifying glass so the watching world can look through the lens of our lives to view the "splendor, brightness, magnificence, excellence, majesty"[2] (glory) of God. We are to be a tool to allow others to

- perceive God as bigger than ever
- see God better
- make God easier to see
- see God in more detail
- make God appear closer
- view God like never before

Then those around us will exclaim "Wow!" "Cool!" "You gotta come see this!" "I never knew God was like that!" The inquisitive will investigate one life situation after another through the lens of our lives.

Paul adds another vantage point for whatever we do: "And whatever you do in word or deed, do all in the name of the Lord Jesus, giving thanks to God the Father through Him" (Col. 3:17 NKJV). This is not adding to our job requirements, but delimiting our process. When we do all "in the name of Jesus," we represent every aspect that is incorporated in the mentioning, hearing, or remembering of His name. For example, if I mentioned the name "Kirk," immediately your mind would be flooded with images, concepts, quotes, and a variety of memories that revolve around your icon of Kirk. Certainly there are behaviors that are not consistent with the name of Kirk. You could never imagine Kirk owning a pet tarantula, for example, since he hates spiders.

When we operate "in the name of Jesus," we are to be consistent with every truth that is incorporated in His attributes. As the Holy Spirit lives in and through us, we will consistently "do all in the name of the Lord Jesus" because we are not operating out of our own resources but are overflowing with His abundant supply. What an astonishing view of God the world would see if all Christians magnified the glory of God in such a fashion!

"Do you have the gift of speaking? Then speak as though God himself were speaking through you. Do you have the gift of helping others? Do it with all the strength and energy that God supplies. Then everything you do will bring glory to God through Jesus Christ. All glory and power to him forever and ever! Amen" (1 Peter 4:11).

Jesus also speaks of bringing glory to God when we ask anything in Jesus' name. "You can ask for anything in my name, and I will do it, so that the Son can bring glory to the Father. Yes, ask me for anything in my name, and I will do it!" (John 14:13–14). Praying in Jesus' name is remembering all the character traits of God, all the ways He has worked in the past, and what a difference it makes that Jesus died and paid for our sins. When we conduct our lives according to everything we know about His character, our expectations will be in line with the reality of who He is, and our hopes will not be disappointed.

Too often we are disappointed with God because He did not respond in a way we thought He should. We place expectations on Him that He has never promised to fulfill. And then in our frustration and disillusionment we whine that God is distant and uncaring. It is true that His ways are incomprehensible, but for some reason we think we have Him all figured out. "Oh, how great are God's riches and wisdom and knowledge! How impossible it is for us to understand his decisions and his ways!" (Rom. 11:33).

"'For I know the plans I have for you,' says the LORD. 'They are plans for good and not for disaster, to give you a future and a hope. In those days when you pray, I will listen. If you look for me wholeheartedly, you will find me. I will be found by you,' says the LORD" (Jer. 29:11–14).

God does not want to hide from you. He desires an intimate relationship with you. So then why do we have to seek? God doesn't work like we expect Him to. We find Him and His answers in the most unlikely places.

> I publicly proclaim bold promises.
>   I do not whisper obscurities in some dark corner.
> I would not have told the people of Israel to seek me
>   if I could not be found.
> I, the LORD, speak only what is true
>   and declare only what is right.
>
> —Isa. 45:19

My (Melanie) Opi (German grandfather) always delighted in the fun tradition of an Easter egg hunt for all ages. For him, Easter was the second most festive holiday of the year. It was celebrated like a mini-Christmas. "Eggs" were hidden for all in attendance. The designated "Easter Bunny" would hide the treasures throughout the yard. Of course chocolates and other treats could be discovered, but gifts were also strategically located. Some were addressed to a specific recipient; others were fair game to all. If you found an egg with a name other than your own on it, you would quietly leave it in its place for the designated owner.

When no more loot could be found, eager hunters would sit to evaluate their bounty. The Easter Bunny would invariably oversee and notice that some prizes had not been claimed. Others would comment, "I saw an egg for you still sitting somewhere." Enthusiastically, the hunter would begin his search again. If the prize still remained undiscovered, an offer of assistance was made.

The assistance was most often orchestrated by my Opi, who was a choir director. The hunter was instructed to begin heading in one direction or another. The singing from the "choir" would become louder or softer depending on whether the hunter was getting closer or farther from the destination. All were elated when the trophy was acquired.

This story illustrates the idea that God does not hide His will from us because He does not want us to know His plans. He desires for us to be active participants in relating to Him. "It is God's privilege to conceal things / and the king's privilege to discover them" (Prov. 25:2). There is great reward in pursuing a goal and attaining what the giver intended for us to have. We must simply look in the right place.

> If any of you lacks wisdom, he should ask God, who gives generously to all without finding fault, and it will be given to him. But when he asks, he must believe and not doubt, because he who doubts is like a wave of the sea, blown and tossed by the wind. That man should not think he will receive anything from the Lord; he is a double-minded man, unstable in all he does.
>
> —James 1:5–8 NIV

Simplify

One of our college professors, Mr. Chuck Hubler, challenged us to consider the concept of Christian priorities. If we followed "But seek first the kingdom of God and His righteousness, and all these things shall be added to you" (Matt. 6:33 NKJV), how would we order our lives? God first? Spouse second? Children third? Job fourth? Everything else falls into place after that? OK. Since there are 24 hours in each day, then if I have God in first place, He gets 12.5 hours of my day. After all, that's more than half. My job generally requires 8 hours a day, and since my spouse has a higher rank than my job, my spouse should have at least 9 hours, and the kids get 8.5 hours. Hmm…That adds up to 38 hours in a day, but I also need sleep! So let's make family second. That includes both my spouse and my kids, and they would get more than my job—8.5 hours per day, which equals 29 hours. Still no sleep.…Let's see. God has to be before my job. My job gets 8 hours, so my family gets 8.5 hours, and God gets 9 hours. Now I'm down to 25.5 hours. I sure am tired....Well, when I'm working, I'm working for my family, so my 8 hours on the job can count as family time, and God would still be in first place if I gave Him 8.5 hours. Hooray! I can get 7.5 hours of sleep and God can be first! What am I going to do with my 8.5 hours with God?

For all the years we have tried to follow that theory, it sounded good, but it's impossible to do! In actuality, the Greek work translated "first" in Matthew 6:33 means "'above all'...which corresponds to the central position which orientation to the kingdom of God has in the proclamation of Jesus. Indeed, πρῶτον is so exclusive here that it carries the implication of 'only.'"[3] How in the world do you do that?

If God were to be above all in our lives with the only central position, He would be everything—in the center. With God in the center of our lives, everything we do involves Him and He influences everything we do. As He lives in and through us, we operate through His enablement to magnify and glorify Him.

God Is Central

Matthew, Mark, and Luke recount what Jesus had to say about becoming a follower of Christ. "Then he said to the crowd, 'If any of you wants to be my follower, you must turn from your selfish ways, take up your cross daily, and follow me'" (Luke 9:23; see also Matt. 16:24; Mark 8:34). When we deny ourselves and turn from our selfish ways, we are to give up anything that pulls us away from God. If we find ourselves caught in the dilemma of deciding between God's ways and anything contrary to God's guidelines, then we are to oppose whatever is tempting us to choose a different path. Remember, God is not trying to hide His plan from you. You can follow step by step what He has revealed in His Word. As we learn to pay attention to the established truths, we can more readily hear what His Spirit whispers to our souls.

To follow Him, we are required to make the necessary sacrifices. We cannot continue to counterfeit the fruit of the Spirit while rejecting God's design for love, joy, and peace. God created us. We cannot conjure up anything better than what He knows we need. We must offer up all our self-contrived dreams that are not His desires for us.

To persist in our selfish ambition and vain conceit we evidence our desire to live independently from Him. The results and consequences of such actions will be fulfilled as He promised.

> But because you are stubborn and refuse to turn from your sin, you are storing up terrible punishment for yourself. For a day of anger is coming, when God's righteous judgment will be revealed. He will judge everyone according to what they have done. He will give eternal life to those who keep on doing good, seeking after the glory and honor and immortality that God offers. But he will pour out his anger and wrath on those who live for themselves, who refuse to obey the truth and instead live lives of wickedness.
>
> —Rom. 2:5–8

Hebrews 4:1–3 elaborates on God's promises for a life that is desperately dependent on Him.

> God's promise of entering his rest still stands, so we ought to tremble with fear that some of you might fail to experience it. For this good news—that God has prepared this rest—has been announced to us just as it was to them. But it did them no good because they didn't share the faith of those who listened to God. For only we who believe can enter his rest. As for the others, God said,

"In my anger I took an oath:
    'They will never enter my place of rest,'"

even though this rest has been ready since he made the world.

Unify

Because it is our job to be in a relationship with Jesus Christ and it is His desire to be in a relationship with us, we must work in unison with Christ as His Holy Spirit moves us to maturity. Moses had the most challenging job of leading the children of Israel into the Promised Land. Moses' mountaintop experience on Mount Sinai soon crashed to the pits of despair when he found that the people had created a golden calf to worship. Despondent, he petitioned the Lord.

> Moses said to the LORD, "You have been telling me, 'Take these people up to the Promised Land.' But you haven't told me whom you will send with me. You call me by name and tell me I have found favor with you. Please, if this is really so, show me your intentions so I will understand you more fully and do exactly what you want me to do. Besides, don't forget that this nation is your very own people."
>
> And the LORD replied, "I will personally go with you, Moses. I will give you rest—everything will be fine for you."
>
> Then Moses said, "If you don't go with us personally, don't let us move a step from this place. If you don't go with us, how will anyone ever know that your people and I have found favor with you? How else will they know we are special and distinct from all other people on the earth?"
>
> And the LORD replied to Moses, "I will indeed do what you have asked, for you have found favor with me, and you are my friend."
>
> —Ex. 33:12–17

When God chose Moses to lead the children of Israel to the Promised Land, He did not intend for Moses to complete the job all by himself. God desired to have a personal relationship with Moses, not just a Savior relationship with the Israelites. When we complain to God, He gives the same response: "I will personally go with you, Moses. I will give you rest—everything will be fine for you." But do we respond as Moses did? "If you don't go with us personally, don't let us move a step from this place." It seems that most often we start running in all directions, trying to find where God wants us to go and what He wants us to do, instead of waiting for Him to go with us personally. If only we would consistently reply, "I will not move a step if You don't go with me."

> In view of all this, make every effort to respond to God's promises. Supplement your faith with a generous provision of moral excellence, and moral excellence with knowledge, and knowledge with self-control, and self-control with patient endurance, and patient endurance with godliness, and godliness with brotherly affection, and brotherly affection with love for everyone.
>
> The more you grow like this, the more productive and useful you will be in your knowledge of our Lord Jesus Christ. But those who fail to develop in this way are shortsighted or blind, forgetting that they have been cleansed from their old sins.
>
> So, dear brothers and sisters, work hard to prove that you really are among those God has called and chosen. Do these things, and you will never fall away. Then God will give you a grand entrance into the eternal Kingdom of our Lord and Savior Jesus Christ.
>
> —2 Peter 1:5–11

Second Peter invites us to collaborate with God in maturing our faith. Jesus works in us through the Holy Spirit, enabling us to embrace the divine character of God. As a result of His enablement, we now have the ability to exhibit His nature. For this reason, we are to exert every effort to complement our faith by following His example.

> Then he added, "Pay close attention to what you hear. The closer you listen, the more understanding you will be given—and you will receive even more. To those who listen to my teaching, more understanding will be given. But for those who are not listening, even what little understanding they have will be taken away from them."
>
> —Mark 4:24–25

As we follow His example we operate with discernment to determine His way. By participating with God we can see what is right versus wrong, what is good versus evil, what is healthy versus dysfunctional, what is truthful versus deceitful, thereby protecting us from the corruption of our self-centered way. We are empowered to live beyond ourselves.

Paul offers his life as an example of how frustrating it is to live outside a desperately dependent relationship with Christ.

> I have discovered this principle of life—that when I want to do what is right, I inevitably do what is wrong. I love God's law with all my heart. But there is another power within me that is at war with my mind. This power makes me a slave to the sin that is still within me. Oh, what a miserable person I am! Who will free me from this life that is dominated by sin and death? Thank God! The answer is in Jesus Christ our Lord.
>
> —Rom. 7:21–25

Only by connecting to Jesus Christ our Lord can we be free from the dominating struggle that threatens to consume us. When we are given a set of rules to follow, our sinful tendency is to rebel and assert our independence. But pursuing God frees us from the control of our sinful selves.

With our agenda no longer at the forefront, we are now freed from the dominance of our desires to therefore follow God consistently and achieve His purpose. A fulfilling relationship emerges as God connects to us, we connect to God, and others experience the overflow of our divinely empowered connection.

We have repeatedly emphasized the fact that God desires an intimate relationship with us. But the choice remains ours as individuals: Will I be desperately dependent? He created me; He cares for me; He knows what is best for me; but will I choose to let Him control every area of my life from His perspective? Will I invite Him to come into my life? Or do I want to hold on to my will and my ways? Am I willing to embrace Jesus to allow Him full reign in my life? If the answer is yes, then Proverbs tells us what to do.

> My child, listen to what I say,
>   and treasure my commands.
> Tune your ears to wisdom,
>   and concentrate on understanding.
> Cry out for insight,
>   and ask for understanding.
> Search for them as you would for silver;
>   seek them like hidden treasures.
> Then you will understand what it means to fear the LORD,
>   and you will gain knowledge of God.

For the Lord grants wisdom!
  From his mouth come knowledge and understanding.
He grants a treasure of common sense to the honest.
  He is a shield to those who walk with integrity.
He guards the paths of the just
  and protects those who are faithful to him.

Then you will understand what is right, just, and fair,
  and you will find the right way to go.
For wisdom will enter your heart,
  and knowledge will fill you with joy.
Wise choices will watch over you.
  Understanding will keep you safe.

—Prov. 2:1–11

He desires to be your God. He is prepared to lead and control every area of your life. He died to be your Savior. He lives to be your sustainer. He offers to be your benefactor. When you genuinely choose to experience the God who is actively pursuing you, you will actively pursue Him.

Jesus makes Himself available and attainable. If we desire a relationship with Him, we may have an abundant life as a result of His grace and mercy. All this is accessible by our desperate dependency on Christ. The most essential discipline of faith is dependency. Our dependency defines the course of all we do.

When we are desperately dependent, our eager search for truth fosters a looming desire to know the heart and mind of God. "Fear of the Lord is the foundation of wisdom. / Knowledge of the Holy One results in good judgment" (Prov. 9:10). Prayer, Bible reading, and church attendance are ways to connect to God. But God did not design these disciplines as an obligation to be completed as a part of our daily routine. Prayer, for example, is the avenue whereby we can talk to God and communicate whatever is on our hearts. We don't need to merely talk to ourselves throughout the day, because we have the privilege of interacting with Him at any given moment for any given reason. "Never stop praying" (1 Thess. 5:17). With eager anticipation we can embark on each new encounter with Him because it affords us the privilege of maturing into Christlikeness. There is no greater goal in life than receiving from His hand what God intends for us to enjoy.

> What can we bring to the LORD?
>> What kind of offerings should we give him?
> Should we bow before God
>> with offerings of yearling calves?
> Should we offer him thousands of rams
>> and ten thousand rivers of olive oil?
> Should we sacrifice our firstborn children
>> to pay for our sins?
>
> No, O people, the LORD has told you what is good,
>> and this is what he requires of you:
> to do what is right, to love mercy,
>> and to walk humbly with your God.
>
> —Mic. 6:6–8

As we live lives that are desperately dependent on Christ, the resulting connection will magnify the Lord. Realizing that our central focus of life is to make Him look wonderful, the dross of the world falls away. Our unified adventure with God supplies purpose and meaning to life. C. S. Lewis wrote, "But look for Christ and you will find Him, and with Him everything else thrown in."[4]

Insight Journal

1. How can I apply these verses to my life?
    "And now, just as you accepted Christ Jesus as your Lord, you must continue to follow him. Let your roots grow down into him, and let your lives be built on him. Then your faith will grow strong in the truth you were taught, and you will overflow with thankfulness.

    "Don't let anyone capture you with empty philosophies and high-sounding nonsense that come from human thinking and from the spiritual powers of this world, rather than from Christ. For in Christ lives all the fullness of God in a human body. So you also are complete through your union with Christ, who is the head over every ruler and authority."

    —Col. 2:6–10

2. If I applied these verses to my life, what would I do differently?
    "Since you have been raised to new life with Christ, set your sights on the realities of heaven, where Christ sits in the place of honor at God's right hand. Think about the things of heaven, not the things of earth. For you died to this life, and your real life is hidden with Christ in God."

    —Col. 3:1–3

3. To magnify/glorify God I must:
4. I know God wants me to:
5. I know I am doing what God wants me to when:

Psalms Prayer Pattern

Hear my prayer, O Lord;
> listen to my plea!
> Answer me because you are faithful and righteous.
Don't put your servant on trial,
> for no one is innocent before you.
My enemy has chased me.
> He has knocked me to the ground
> and forces me to live in darkness like those in the grave.
I am losing all hope;
> I am paralyzed with fear.
I remember the days of old.
> I ponder all your great works
> and think about what you have done.
I lift my hands to you in prayer.
> I thirst for you as parched land thirsts for rain. *Interlude*

Come quickly, Lord, and answer me,
> for my depression deepens.
Don't turn away from me,
> or I will die.
Let me hear of your unfailing love each morning,
> for I am trusting you.
Show me where to walk,
> for I give myself to you.
Rescue me from my enemies, Lord;
> I run to you to hide me.
Teach me to do your will,
> for you are my God.
May your gracious Spirit lead me forward
> on a firm footing.
For the glory of your name, O Lord, preserve my life.
> Because of your faithfulness, bring me out of this distress.
In your unfailing love, silence all my enemies
> and destroy all my foes,
> for I am your servant.

—Ps. 143

CHAPTER 11

Living in the Truth

FROM THE VERY beginning of humanity's fall into sin, we have been in bondage to the lie that we can live independently of God and thrive by depending on our own abilities and resources. This distorted view of reality perverts everything that is true and righteous into a culture of lies. We will not accept anything we do not believe is true, but what we believe is not really true. With our skewed perception of God, our reality views Him as one who is not invested in our best interests and who deprives us of our rightful pleasures. Or we may even believe God is OK with whatever we want to pursue because He ultimately wants us to be happy, right? To be free from the perversion that results in our bondage, we must live in God's truth.

A friend called, stating, "I feel so lost, so much in a hole, so disconnected from God. I feel I am completely alone in a void. How do I find Jesus relevant to this? Do I just believe the truth?" In spite of his sarcasm, he knew the right answer. His wrong attitude prevented him from being empowered by the freedom that comes from recognizing God's truth as capable of resolving each life situation.

Revelation 3 elaborates on God's perspective concerning our lack of commitment and self-deception.

> I know all the things you do, that you are neither hot nor cold. I wish that you were one
> or the other! But since you are like lukewarm water, neither hot nor cold, I will spit you

out of my mouth! You say, "I am rich. I have everything I want. I don't need a thing!" And you don't realize that you are wretched and miserable and poor and blind and naked.

—Rev. 3:15–17

God invites us to choose commitment and share in a relationship with Him as we walk in His truth. "Look! I stand at the door and knock. If you hear my voice and open the door, I will come in, and we will share a meal together as friends" (Rev. 3:20).

In chapter 3 of this book we stated that, unfortunately, we must still contend with the nature of sin resident in our lives. But, gratefully, at the point of salvation we are blessed with a new set of options. No longer are we bound by the power of sin in our lives. We may now choose from His abundant resources and allow His divine enablement to personally empower our lives. How can we live in this victory?

The Call of Truth

Truth is comprised of principles, precepts, and promises of God that empower life with the strength of God. Although God's law is written in our hearts, we must make the choice to believe God's truth by accepting His reality as fact. Yet just knowing God's truth as fact will not change our lives until we believe by faith and appropriate God's truth in the course of our living. It is not until truth shapes our choices and molds our behavior, sculpting us into the image of Jesus, that we may say we believe. Do we really believe what we say we believe about God so that it permeates our lives and defines our actions?

> For merely listening to the law doesn't make us right with God. It is obeying the law that makes us right in his sight. Even Gentiles, who do not have God's written law, show that they know his law when they instinctively obey it, even without having heard it. They demonstrate that God's law is written in their hearts, for their own conscience and thoughts either accuse them or tell them they are doing right.

—Rom. 2:13–15

Perversion, the enemy of truth, is the means by which Satan distorts and deceives in order to blind and to bind. Individuals are bound to lies, constituting the spiritual war between perversion and truth. This is the battleground upon which the Holy Spirit fights for our souls.

But we are not puppets; we are willing participants who choose to either walk in truth or perversion. At any given moment we are either moving away from perversion to the truth, or we are moving from truth to perversion. Too often we are torn between Satan's perversions and the truth of God that states we are complete in Christ. The restraining force of the Holy Spirit in our lives reminds us that God is sufficient, while Satan whispers in our ear that self-gratification can fill the emptiness: "I believe my flesh can make me happy, but God won't let me have what I want!"

Habitually we choose to dwell in the comfort zone of believing the lie that we can be complete without God. But this self-sufficient delusion only reinforces our bondage of living in servitude to our flesh. Oppression erodes our emotional fortitude and leads to death in all areas of life, because death is the result of living independently of Christ. "Then why do these people stay on their self-destructive path?.../ They cling tightly to their lies / and will not turn around" (Jer. 8:5).

Perversion traps the unrepentant in the pathology of the sin nature. Regrettably, the deluded self-righteous soul chooses empowerment apart from Christ's redemptive process and becomes ensnared by legalism or is lulled into leniency. Neither excessive adherence to the law nor subscribing only to the permissive, merciful, and tolerant attributes of God encompasses God's design for a relationship with His children. God does hold us accountable for deviance from His divine standard so we may have fellowship with His holiness. He also offers merciful forgiveness to the repentant that authentically choose Christ's way, instead of continuing to follow their own desires. Remember, God's design places Him at the center of our existence and makes Him responsible for our physical life, quality of life, and eternal life. Man's desire, however, places himself at the center of his own existence, and he expects God to revolve around him while he pursues his own inclinations for physical life, quality of life, and eternal life.

One deluded soul was so convinced of his deception that he stated, "I don't believe God is OK with what I am doing; but when I die and stand before God, I do believe I can explain it to Him and He will be OK with it." "Well then, should we keep on sinning so that God can show us more and more of his wonderful grace? Of course not! Since we have died to sin, how can we continue to live in it?" (Rom. 6:1–2).

The self-sufficient soul seeks empowerment through God substitutes. Every attempt to find empowerment through any means other than Christ's redemptive process through Christ's redemptive work results in self-delusion and destruction. It is only through finding Christ relevant to every aspect of our lives that we can be freed from the power of sin.

At the point of salvation, we accept Christ's full payment of our sin debt that resulted from living in perversion. But only through Christ's redemptive process can the pathology of the sin nature be defeated through truth. Please notice it is a process! We must continuously choose God's truth and deny Satan's lies and perversion. By embracing Christ's empowering redemptive process, we choose Christ-centeredness that results in freedom and abundant life. The nature of God's truth moves all to encounter Christ as centrally relevant to their lives.

Jesus said, "I have come that they may have life, and that they may have it more abundantly" (John 10:10 NKJV).

"Jesus answered, 'I am the way and the truth and the life. No one comes to the Father except through me'" (John 14:6 NIV).

We need to break the power of perversion by embracing truth until it permeates every aspect of our being and we attain Christlikeness. This is accomplished by responding to the movement of the Holy Spirit—the call of truth.

> Wisdom shouts in the streets.
>> She cries out in the public square.
> She calls to the crowds along the main street,
>> to those gathered in front of the city gate:
> "How long, you simpletons,
>> will you insist on being simpleminded?
> How long will you mockers relish your mocking?
>> How long will you fools hate knowledge?
> Come and listen to my counsel.
> I'll share my heart with you
>> and make you wise."
>
> —Prov. 1:20–23

Trauma of Truth

In modern-day Christianity people are trying to change truth, rather than have truth change them. As we acquire a more complete perspective of God's values, we gain a more comprehensive insight of how desperately we fall short of His design. When we connect to our sinfulness in the light of God's holiness, the Holy Spirit transforms our hearts through the trauma of truth. Consequently, our orientation to God is transformed,

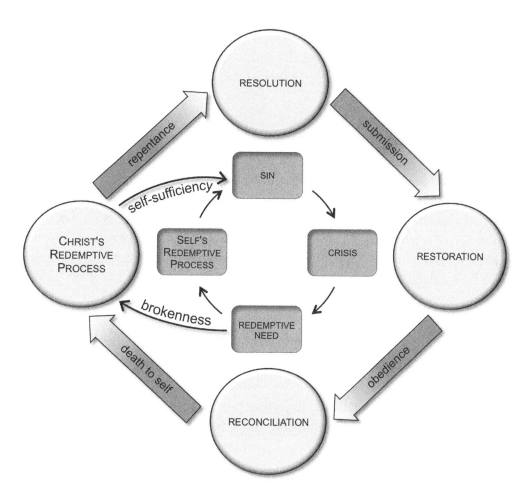

The Solution

our perspective of God changes, and so does our perception of people, positions, and possessions. The Holy Spirit reveals God's truth, we encounter God's truth, and our response is to be traumatized by His truth.

It is impossible to move from perversion to living in truth, without brokenness that results from the trauma of truth. Brokenness is the willingness to give up our willfulness. As the Holy Spirit reveals God's perspective to our deceived hearts, we come face to face with the tragic truth that we are sinful souls. We are alienated enemies of God with no hope. The resulting grief can produce healthy, therapeutic guilt, shame, and fear as we begin to interact with and mourn these truths. Through the trauma of truth, godly sorrow produces a spiritual disruption of the heart that leads to the reordering of our souls, maturing us into Christlikeness. This productive pain reveals that my value system is changing. I want to be different. This is the foundation of repentance. Or I may choose to reside with the toxic guilt, shame, and fear of the sin nature.

> The pain caused you to repent and change your ways. It was the kind of sorrow God wants his people to have, so you were not harmed by us in any way. For the kind of sorrow God wants us to experience leads us away from sin and results in salvation. There's no regret for that kind of sorrow. But worldly sorrow, which lacks repentance, results in spiritual death.
>
> Just see what this godly sorrow produced in you! Such earnestness, such concern to clear yourselves, such indignation, such alarm, such longing to see me, such zeal, and such a readiness to punish wrong. You showed that you have done everything necessary to make things right.
>
> —2 Cor. 7:9–11

There are only two options—people will respond by receiving truth or rejecting truth. To receive the truth means we are allowing the Holy Spirit's work to be solidified in our lives; the changes are becoming permanent. God's work takes hold in our hearts as we abandon self and walk in brokenness. Rejecting God's truth produces a hardened heart that rebels against the Holy Spirit's efforts to bring us to brokenness.

It is the nature of truth to build or destroy. Because God is Creator of all, His truth undergirds all. Foundations are built or crumble as the direct result of His establishment. His truth maintains accountability and brings consequences into our lives, both negative and positive. As we follow God's truth, His promised blessings result. If we neglect God's truth, His promised destruction results. "The way of the LORD is a stronghold to those with integrity, / but it destroys the wicked" (Prov. 10:29).

> Be careful then, dear brothers and sisters. Make sure that your own hearts are not evil and unbelieving, turning you away from the living God. You must warn each other every day, while it is still "today," so that none of you will be deceived by sin and hardened against God. For if we are faithful to the end, trusting God just as firmly as when we first believed, we will share in all that belongs to Christ. Remember what it says:

"Today when you hear his voice,
    don't harden your hearts
    as Israel did when they rebelled."

—Heb. 3:12–15

Transformation by Truth

Living in the truth is the process of divine transformation where God changes me. The permeation of God's truth in my life alters all aspects of my being—what I believe, how I think, what I feel, how I behave, and the choices I make. I am made new. "My old self has been crucified with Christ. It is no longer I who live, but Christ lives in me. So I live in this earthly body by trusting in the Son of God, who loved me and gave himself for me" (Gal. 2:20).

Our violating God's law and usurping His authority required the death penalty. The sinless Son of God died to satisfy the justice of God. Although Christ was the one who was crucified, God views His sacrifice as satisfying His righteous demands on our behalf. Therefore what Christ has done for us, we have done through Him. "My old self has been crucified with Christ." Christ completed what we were not qualified to do for ourselves. We could not make atonement for our sin. We could only be punished for eternity. What He did, He did for us. Our sins were judged on the cross. Our sinful selves died.

So now there is no condemnation for those who belong to Christ Jesus. And because you belong to him, the power of the life-giving Spirit has freed you from the power of sin that leads to death. The law of Moses was unable to save us because of the weakness of our sinful nature. So God did what the law could not do. He sent his own Son in a body like the bodies we sinners have. And in that body God declared an end to sin's control over us by giving his Son as a sacrifice for our sins. He did this so that the just requirement of the law would be fully satisfied for us, who no longer follow our sinful nature but instead follow the Spirit.

—Rom. 8:1–4

As the result of being crucified with Christ, we possess the divine ability to live new lives. "Since we have been united with him in his death, we will also be raised to life as he was. We know that our old sinful selves were crucified with Christ so that sin might lose its power in our lives. We are no longer slaves to sin. For when we died with Christ we were set free from the power of sin" (Rom. 6:5–7).

If we receive by faith the gift that is offered to us, we can also receive the benefits that are applied to us. Christ's completed work enables us to be empowered because "Christ lives in me" (Gal. 2:20). The application of salvation provides divinely enabled abilities. We can actually die to self because the Holy Spirit resides in us. Without the Holy Spirit we have no ability to please God. Perhaps we think we could perform good deeds, but "We are all infected and impure with sin. / When we display our righteous deeds, / they are nothing but filthy rags" (Isa. 64:6). Through His divine enablement, we can now be personally empowered to behave in a way that pleases God.

We may have a vast knowledge of the Bible, but if this knowledge has never changed us it is because we do not believe what we know to be true. When we believe, we act on what we know is certain. "Faith is the confidence that what we hope for will actually happen; it gives us assurance about things we cannot see" (Heb. 11:1). It does not require complete comprehension. Absolute understanding is not a necessity. What is essential is that we trust and follow in God's way. "You will hear a word spoken behind you, saying, 'This is the correct way, walk in it,' whether you are heading to the right or the left" (Isa. 30:21).

Our inability to trust reveals that we do not believe God at His word. It is imperative that we acknowledge and confess our unbelief. Authentically facing the reality that we do not believe God results in the trauma of truth that challenges our value system. When we acknowledge our inadequacy, genuine concern for ourselves motivates us to seek God for help. "Unless your faith is firm, / I cannot make you stand firm" (Isa. 7:9).

Those who choose to receive God's truth and enter into Christ's redemptive process will move to repentance. Repentance is that place where we turn from our philosophy of self-centeredness to Christ-centeredness. It is opting to live and do life God's way and giving up our self-sufficiency.

Those who continue in deception may attempt a ritual of repentance. With no true heart change, they may go through the motions commonly deemed consistent with repentance such as crying, revealing sinfulness, asking for forgiveness, going to the altar, making promises to be different, or even a renewed religious fervor. But these actions are merely playing "good" as these individuals attempt to feign something they do not possess. They are not actually seeking to be free from the domination of sin, but merely free from the consequences of their sin. Deceptive individuals hope to project the virtue of godly change while remaining in their philosophy of self-centeredness. Through an elaborate ruse they attempt to regain power and control so they can once again manipulate trust to exploit others. But as we give up our willfulness to God and relinquish ourselves unreservedly to Christ, submission to God's authority, obedience to God's design, and death to our selfish desires will result.

> "Yet they act so pious!
> They come to the Temple every day
>   and seem delighted to learn all about me.
> They act like a righteous nation
>   that would never abandon the laws of its God.
> They ask me to take action on their behalf,
>   pretending they want to be near me.
> 'We have fasted before you!' they say.
>   'Why aren't you impressed?
> We have been very hard on ourselves,
>   and you don't even notice it!'
>
> "I will tell you why!" I respond.
>   "It's because you are fasting to please yourselves....
> You humble yourselves
>   by going through the motions of penance,
> bowing your heads
>   like reeds bending in the wind.
> You dress in burlap
>   and cover yourselves with ashes.
> Is this what you call fasting?
>   Do you really think this will please the LORD?"

—Isa. 58:2–3, 5

Often evil pretends to be good. When our profession of faith is not congruent with our possession of Christ, sin gets normalized through deceptive rationalizations. The expression of evil is then disguised in the charade of goodness. Evil may present itself with a demeanor of goodness to the point we wonder, *How could such a good person do this?* Then we must look deeper at the possibility that the alleged goodness is merely a facade to disguise evil. "Make sure that the light you think you have is not actually darkness" (Luke 11:35). "And if the light you think you have is actually darkness, how deep that darkness is!" (Matt. 6:23).

Some may lead others to believe that their basic heart is good, with only random aspects of sinfulness. Thus their unhealthiness is promptly dismissed as soon as convenient, and their evil becomes normalized. After all, we are all going to make mistakes, right? "'Don't scheme against each other. Stop your love of telling lies that you swear are the truth. I hate all these things,' says the LORD" (Zech. 8:17).

Others complain that it is just too hard to do what God is asking. When we protest, "It's too hard," we are actually stating that God is not keeping His promise to enable us. Even in Old Testament times, the people protested that God's ways were too difficult, and so they attempted to adjust His standards of holiness. This was God's response:

> "But you dishonor my name with your actions. By bringing contemptible food, you are saying it's all right to defile the Lord's table. You say, 'It's too hard to serve the LORD,' and you turn up your noses at my commands," says the LORD of Heaven's Armies. "Think of it! Animals that are stolen and crippled and sick are being presented as offerings! Should I accept from you such offerings as these?" asks the LORD…"For I am a great king," says the LORD of Heaven's Armies, "and my name is feared among the nations!"
> —Mal. 1:12–14

So how is it that we manage to believe we do not have to give God our best? Why are we convinced that He is asking something of us that is too difficult? When will we choose to believe God's truth instead of falling for Satan's deceptions? Moses was whining, too. "And the LORD told Moses, 'When you arrive back in Egypt, go to Pharaoh and perform all the miracles I have empowered you to do'" (Ex. 4:21). In the midst of all our weakness we can rest assured that God will empower us to accomplish what He desires of us.

When we enter Christ's redemptive process through brokenness, our repentance leads us to the resolution of our guilt, shame, and fear, so we willingly choose submission to His process. Satan has perverted the concept of submission, similarly to the concept of dependency, so we believe it is something to be avoided. Through submission we yield our hearts to God's will and our wills to God's heart. This surrender creates a reciprocal harmony of fellowship between God and us. Together we walk step by step with the heartbeat of God. We do not have to come up with our own plans or follow our own processes; we can compliantly follow His way. This submission establishes the path of restoration to love, joy, and peace, and produces grateful obedience.

Obedience is the place where divine enablement meets with personal empowerment. Our desires are not merely to rigidly do what God wants us to do, but to fervently seek to know and pursue His will. Our motivation for living is to connect to God in a vibrant relationship where we are studying His Word and communing in prayer and following His design. This yearning for prayer and assimilating the Scriptures is for the purpose of understanding His heart and applying His principles to every aspect of our lives, realizing that His designs are perfect. It is our responsibility to allow God's Word to infiltrate the void created when we yielded our independence to God. We bow before God, willing to be governed by His sovereignty.

"So are you saying all I need to do is read my Bible and everything will be fine?"

Actually, if you personalize God's truth contained in your Bible, you will be transformed. The relevance of His life-changing truth is all that is needed for life and living. The One who designed us knows exactly what it takes for us to live an abundant life. Why do we think we can come up with a better plan? He had it all figured out before He even created Adam and Eve. It is simply our responsibility to surrender to His design by walking in His way. We accomplish this by believing and acting on God's truth. His Word is an all-encompassing record of the ways we can trust Him.

"Since you have heard about Jesus and have learned the truth that comes from him, throw off your old sinful nature and your former way of life, which is corrupted by lust and deception. Instead, let the Spirit renew your thoughts and attitudes. Put on your new nature, created to be like God—truly righteous and holy" (Eph. 4:21–24). The admonition here is not to merely make better decisions, but to make empowered choices to mature into Christlikeness.

Because we have been reconciled to God, through Jesus, by the Holy Spirit, we may now die to self so that our ways become His ways. His divine enablement empowers us to sacrifice anything that interferes with our following Christ, whether it is influential people, strategic positions, or satisfying possessions. As we die to self, we can suffer through confrontation, ridicule, persecution, deprivation, and oppression for the cause of following Christ. As corpses who have been revived by Christ, we can face anything that opposes our following Christ. Although our flesh may suffer consequences, we abandon the desires to promote or preserve self. Whatever the sacrifice and whatever we must endure, we do not have to be influenced by our sinful selves, because we choose Christ's redemptive process instead of self's redemptive process.

Since the Spirit of God and the spirit of sin are at war within us (Gal. 5:17), self must be conquered. As we choose dependency on God's Holy Spirit, His Spirit will combat and defeat the resident hostile forces that are against God. Through repentance, the fleshly resistance is rendered inoperative. A new foundation of resurrected freedom triumphantly allows us to embrace a new life in Christ. The fallen regime of self should no longer influence our minds, hearts, or souls since we consistently choose to be part of Christ's redemptive process. We may still choose the path of self-sufficiency that will lead us once again into self's redemptive process. God's truth and love, however, will continuously draw us back to the victory we experienced while abiding in Christ's redemptive process.

Submission, obedience, and death to self are the means through which the Holy Spirit postures our souls to fight the sinfulness of our hearts. Yielding to His transforming work matures us to Christlikeness. Although the trauma of truth may be painful, God calls us with His truth to redeem us from the miseries of life. It is vital that we receive the convicting power of truth and allow this intrusion to accomplish His work, thereby transforming us into His likeness. To turn a deaf ear is to shut out the life-giving opportunities God wishes to undertake. God disrupts our lives so He may redesign our souls. "Through the power of the Holy Spirit who lives within us, carefully guard the precious truth that has been entrusted to you" (2 Tim. 1:14).

Insight Journal

1. How is Jesus relevant to the situation I am struggling with today?
2. Prayerfully discern: What lies am I believing that keep me from an intimate relationship with Christ?
3. I was traumatized when I realized:
4. I need to repent of:
5. Write a personal psalm to pour out your heart to God.

Psalms Prayer Pattern

Have mercy on me, O God,
  because of your unfailing love.
Because of your great compassion,
  blot out the stain of my sins.
Wash me clean from my guilt.
  Purify me from my sin.
For I recognize my rebellion;
  it haunts me day and night.
Against you, and you alone, have I sinned;
  I have done what is evil in your sight.
You will be proved right in what you say,
  and your judgment against me is just.
For I was born a sinner—
  yes, from the moment my mother conceived me.
But you desire honesty from the womb,
  teaching me wisdom even there.

Purify me from my sins, and I will be clean;
  wash me, and I will be whiter than snow.
Oh, give me back my joy again;
  you have broken me—
  now let me rejoice.
Don't keep looking at my sins.
  Remove the stain of my guilt.
Create in me a clean heart, O God.
  Renew a loyal spirit within me.
Do not banish me from your presence,
  and don't take your Holy Spirit from me.

Restore to me the joy of your salvation,
    and make me willing to obey you.
Then I will teach your ways to rebels,
    and they will return to you.
Forgive me for shedding blood, O God who saves;
    then I will joyfully sing of your forgiveness.
Unseal my lips, O Lord,
    that my mouth may praise you.

You do not desire a sacrifice, or I would offer one.
    You do not want a burnt offering.
The sacrifice you desire is a broken spirit.
    You will not reject a broken and repentant heart, O God.
Look with favor on Zion and help her;
    rebuild the walls of Jerusalem.
Then you will be pleased with sacrifices offered in the right spirit—
    with burnt offerings and whole burnt offerings.
    Then bulls will again be sacrificed on your altar.

—Ps. 51

CHAPTER 12

Choosing to Be Desperately Dependent

PERHAPS YOU CAN recall a little of the turmoil that invaded your teenage years. Engulfed in a multiplicity of struggles, we floundered to establish our identity. We grappled with a variety of fundamental philosophical questions that have plagued human existence: Who am I? Am I lovable? Where am I going? Because I was created to be dependent, I need someone to tell me who I am. I want someone to label me as lovable. I require someone to guide me. Whomever or whatever I allow to validate these issues establishes my identity. The defining force of my life becomes my god. Daily I choose to be desperately dependent on God, or a God substitute.

Who Am I?

Man was created as a harmonious being. He connected in unity with all exactly as God designed. "Then God looked over all he had made, and he saw that it was very good!" (Gen. 1:31). But when Adam and Eve decided God's design was not adequate, humanity was propelled into a continuous search for completion. We are searching for what was lost—our identity.

Identity is basic to all humans, and our names are foundational to our personal identity. It is usual to have at least an assumed surname at birth. Then comes the arduous undertaking of determining a baby's unique name. This vital task involves considerable energy, as all possible options and combinations are explored until the parents determine the appropriate designation fitting and worthy of someone so special. Authors struggle when naming their characters as they contemplate the characters' individuality, including where they come from and their role in the story. To enhance the unique identity of our personal names we add designations that indicate relationship, accomplishments, and status, such as Mr., Mrs., Rev., Dr., Lt., Col., etc. Authority belongs to those who confer names, and names indicate the significance of what they describe.

I (Kirk) remember my first traumatic encounter with my name. By the time I was four years old, I had enough social interaction with my extended family to know I was not being accepted as their equal. One day I stood by the window of our small house, crying. I remember saying over and over, "I hate my name. I hate my name. I hate my name." Mama, concerned by my actions, came to me and asked, "Kirk, what's the matter?" I looked at her and then back out the window. "I hate my name. Why did you name me Kirk? Why couldn't you have given me a good name—a name starting with R like Ronnie, Randy, or Mark? Then everyone would like me." At this early age I assumed the reason my cousins did not accept me as their equal was because of my name, who I was. This was my simple way of expressing my belief that something was wrong with me. My name must be ugly. That had to be the explanation. Their rejection must be about who I am.

Much to the dismay of my father, my mother wanted to name me Kirk because she was enamored with Kirk Douglas, the movie star. Dad protested and asserted that I would be named after him; thus, John. Mama, in her countermove proclaimed, "His first name will be John and his middle name will be Kirk." As Dad yielded, Mom added this caveat, emphatically announcing, "But he will be called Kirk." In spite of the confusion and conflict between my parents, I am astounded that my name perfectly parallels God's call on my life. John, meaning *sent by God*, and Kirk meaning *church dweller*. In the midst of the domestic chaos, God's sovereign love was at work, continuously attesting, "I love you and I have a plan for you."

Names incorporate major significance in Scripture. The very first name recorded in the Bible is God. "In the beginning God created the heavens and the earth" (Gen. 1:1). Here God is translated from the Hebrew *'elohim*. This name of supremacy expresses who God is, His identity. The name Adam is translated from the Hebrew word for *man*. Hence, Adam being the first man is simply called *man*, depicting who he was. All through the Old Testament we encounter names specifically revealing something about a person: Abraham, Sarah, Isaac, Jacob.

But names such as Abraham, Sarah, Isaac, and Jacob not only incorporate their character; God named and renamed individuals to reflect His purpose in their lives.

We find God assigning names directly to people, as in the case of John and Jesus, or renaming them while commissioning them to a ministry, as in Peter and Paul. God also uses names to declare purpose, to designate plight, or to delimit position, as in the names of the prophets.

Colossians says, "All things were created by him and for him" (1:16 NIV). Therefore "to all who believed him and accepted him, he gave the right to become children of God" (John 1:12). "See how very much our Father loves us, for he calls us his children, and that is what we are!" (1 John 3:1).

> Dear children, don't let anyone deceive you about this: When people do what is right, it shows that they are righteous, even as Christ is righteous. But when people keep on sinning, it shows that they belong to the devil, who has been sinning since the beginning. But the Son of God came to destroy the works of the devil. Those who have been born into God's family do not make a practice of sinning, because God's life is in them. So they can't keep on sinning, because they are children of God. So now we can tell who are children of God and who are children of the devil. Anyone who does not live righteously and does not love other believers does not belong to God.
>
> —1 John 3:7–10

> Everyone who believes that Jesus is the Christ has become a child of God. And everyone who loves the Father loves his children, too. We know we love God's children if we love God and obey his commandments. Loving God means keeping his commandments, and his commandments are not burdensome. For every child of God defeats this evil world, and we achieve this victory through our faith. And who can win this battle against the world? Only those who believe that Jesus is the Son of God.
>
> —1 John 5:1–5

"We know that God's children do not make a practice of sinning, for God's Son holds them securely, and the evil one cannot touch them. We know that we are children of God and that the world around us is under the control of the evil one" (1 John 5:18–19).

The very essence of our identity is interwoven with God Himself. Because God created us, we exist for Him. He desires to adopt us as His children, so that He can name us. Why, then, would we not naturally yearn for Him? The innate desire to be connected with God has been perverted by Satan, subverting our search for Him. Instead we crave for people, positions, and possessions to validate our identity when God has already supplied the needed essentials of love, significance, and security. God wants us to be complete in the person of Christ, the position of His child, and the possession of His righteousness. His love tells us, "You are valued." As His children, we have significance that states, "You have purpose." Because of His righteousness we have security that declares, "You are safe." The quest proceeds with hopes of fulfillment, satisfaction, and completion so we may experience joy and peace. Our identity is bestowed upon us when we choose to embrace truth or succumb to the lies.

Am I Lovable?

A continual skirmish rages as a diversity of options vies for the lofted position of determining who we are perceived to be. Who or what will dictate whether we are loved, significant, or secure? What person will verify that we are cared for? What position will confirm us as valuable? What possession will identify us as worthy?

Every person possesses within his or her heart a completion scenario that delimits what would produce the ultimate fulfillment and satisfaction. This experience would represent the greatest encounter in life. Beyond this, nothing could be better. Our completion scenario is created out of a synthesis of our orientation to God, what we value, and what we think and feel. This completion scenario motivates desire and gives direction to our behavioral pursuits that are reinforced through immediate gratification. It is here within our very own version of our completion scenario that we seek to be validated by our God substitutes.

We are incapable of establishing our own identity. Therefore we need someone other than ourselves to validate us. God's view of life dictates that He is the only one qualified to be our validating source. It is through God's love for us that we receive His validation, establishing that we are lovable, significant, and secure. This God-centered identity leads to completion and fulfillment in Him.

Within our lives we each possess a sacred "God place"—that place designed by God for God. Only He has the right to occupy this position in our lives. From this God place He rules over our souls and replenishes our hearts with His validating love, while establishing our identity. When any other entity occupies this place, we are guilty of idolatry. The Old Testament is replete with warnings and consequences that result when idols invade the lives of God's chosen people. Although we may dismiss these passages because they are often connected with the pagan gods of Baal or Asherah, these admonitions also apply to modern life where we continuously allow other entities to fill our God place and dictate our lives. Any substitution for God we permit to establish our identity, love, significance, or security is an idol. These counterfeits break the heart of God. He aches as He watches our foolish endeavors to find completion in our lives through empty alternatives.

This is what the LORD says—Israel's King and Redeemer, the LORD of Heaven's Armies:

"I am the First and the Last;
    there is no other God.
Who is like me?
    Let him step forward and prove to you his power.
Let him do as I have done since ancient times
    when I established a people and explained its future.
Do not tremble; do not be afraid.
    Did I not proclaim my purposes for you long ago?
You are my witnesses—is there any other God?
    No! There is no other Rock—not one!"

How foolish are those who manufacture idols.
    These prized objects are really worthless.
The people who worship idols don't know this,
    so they are all put to shame.
Who but a fool would make his own god—
    an idol that cannot help him one bit?
All who worship idols will be disgraced
    along with all these craftsmen—mere humans—
    who claim they can make a god.
They may all stand together,
    but they will stand in terror and shame.

The blacksmith stands at his forge to make a sharp tool,
    pounding and shaping it with all his might.
His work makes him hungry and weak.
    It makes him thirsty and faint.

Then the wood-carver measures a block of wood
    and draws a pattern on it.
He works with chisel and plane
    and carves it into a human figure.
He gives it human beauty
    and puts it in a little shrine.
He cuts down cedars;
    he selects the cypress and the oak;
he plants the pine in the forest
    to be nourished by the rain.
Then he uses part of the wood to make a fire.
    With it he warms himself and bakes his bread.
Then—yes, it's true—he takes the rest of it
    and makes himself a god to worship!
He makes an idol
    and bows down in front of it!
He burns part of the tree to roast his meat
    and to keep himself warm.
    He says, "Ah, that fire feels good."
Then he takes what's left
    and makes his god: a carved idol!
He falls down in front of it,
    worshiping and praying to it.
"Rescue me!" he says.
    "You are my god!"

Such stupidity and ignorance!
    Their eyes are closed, and they cannot see.
    Their minds are shut, and they cannot think.
The person who made the idol never stops to reflect,
    "Why, it's just a block of wood!
I burned half of it for heat
    and used it to bake my bread and roast my meat.
How can the rest of it be a god?
    Should I bow down to worship a piece of wood?"

The poor, deluded fool feeds on ashes.

    He trusts something that can't help him at all.

Yet he cannot bring himself to ask,

    "Is this idol that I'm holding in my hand a lie?"

—Isa. 44:6–20

Triangle Tool

When we live independently from God we search for a substitute as our validating source. Without a desperate dependency on Him we establish a counterfeit connection with people, positions, and possessions in our pursuit for validation. We extract love from illicit relationships to prove that we are lovable, to establish our significance, and to enable us to feel secure. But in actuality we suffer loss because people, positions, and possessions are incapable of fulfilling us. Ultimately we are left unfulfilled, dissatisfied, and incomplete as the result of pursuing God substitutes. The delusional sense of satisfaction that stimulates and sedates eventually fades and we are left wanting more. In our vain attempts we explore other counterfeits that may promise temporary contentment, but only provide mutually satisfying exploitation and manipulation to empower our identity.

This is how Joel tells his story.

I have been a Christian since the age of five. I had been very active in church my whole life. But there were two things I wanted out of life. Since kindergarten I wanted to be married and I wanted to be a soldier. I was actually listed in the city newspaper on Valentine's Day for having the most girlfriends in my school, in kindergarten, because that's what I've always wanted—a relationship with a special woman. I believed there was a person out there who would complete me and that I could complete her.

I was introduced to a beautiful, wonderful woman and within a year asked her to marry me. I found the full realm of everything that interdependence had to offer. She was drop-dead gorgeous and made me feel loveable, significant, and secure. I attained my goal.

I also believed my job could give me identity. So I signed up to be a soldier at the age of seventeen (actually, my parents had to sign me in through the Delayed Entry Program). I can't even describe how I felt when I graduated basic training. I had made it. This was my purpose in life. The military. Strong. Proud. Full of honor. I had a place to belong. Kids looked up to me. People thanked me. I was honored. I had love, significance, and security. I had it all.

Because my title of soldier was in my God place, I sacrificed myself for my god. Physically I was pushed by my unit and pushed myself to the point that I sustained many permanent injuries, and for a short time I couldn't even walk. After cycling through recovery and re-injury, I continued to drive myself even with my limitations. Following many visits to doctor's offices, emergency rooms, and twelve surgeries, the military said I was no longer fit for service. At twenty-six years of age I was medically retired from the only career I ever wanted. I was filled with anger, frustration, and pain.

But no matter how bad life got, I was convinced I would be OK, because I still had what really completed me, my wife. People were awestruck by our marriage. Friends admired us and were jealous of our relationship. I'd like to say I forgot about God because

I figured that since I was a Christian He would just bless what I wanted. The truth is, He just wasn't my priority.

Then one of us was no longer interested in "till death do us part." To say I was crushed would be like saying the ocean is a drop of water on a small pile of dirt. Emptiness resulted.

But that didn't mean God took His rightful place. That wasn't what I really wanted. What does it matter if God loves me? My wife doesn't love me. I can't serve in my beloved military anymore. I was empty. There was no human love that mattered, no value, no worth, no purpose, no security, no fulfillment. Nothing mattered, nothing was safe, and nothing was secure. There was nothing to keep me going, no reason for living.

Although God had been God all my life, there was little to no evidence of that in my life. I had dedicated my existence to the idolatry of God substitutes, depending on something that's not God. Because God is who He is, He can bring good out of evil. But that doesn't mean He will give back our God substitutes. In His proper place God can foster love, value, worth, security, and significance.

God will meet us in our pain if we allow Him to. To be honest, I'm not so sure God doesn't welcome pain in our lives. Not because He's sadistic or cruel, but because He knows He's big enough to handle it, and He is enough to bring us through it. The pain just happens to give God a very tangible opportunity to prove it.

God's love will do what you can't fathom. God values me. My life has worth. His love fosters security. God's got me. I fully expect to go through more hard times in my life, but God will be there before them, after them, and most importantly through them, and He will provide what is necessary for my life. I must evaluate my life and my responses to what happens in life. I should be concerned and afraid if He is not filling the God place in my life. I must continuously beg Him to protect me from what I am and weed out the nonessentials that desire to be idols in my life.

Joel looked to people, positions, and possessions to empower love, significance, and security in his life. His gods enabled him to feel complete and contented for a time. But it is the compulsion of any of us to become reliant on whomever we reverence. And when what we reverence becomes the defining entity in our lives, our god, we live in service to what will ultimately disappoint.

Jesus said, "If you want to be my disciple, you must hate everyone else by comparison—your father and mother, wife and children, brothers and sisters—yes, even your own life. Otherwise, you cannot be my disciple" (Luke 14:26). The God place of our souls is designed for Jesus. Boundaries should be built around this sacred place to assure that none other but Christ resides there. It should be guarded by our fear of God with our appropriate view of God serving as the sentinel. The highest of all that is lofty should be ascribed to Jesus so that He attracts in full our hearts, minds, and souls, capturing our strength with the truth of His glory and virtue. Then Jesus becomes central because He is preeminent. We come to see Him in truth, as He actually is—Lord, Savior, lover of our souls, champion of our hearts.

We first establish our identification with Jesus through the salvation of our souls, the sanctification of our hearts, and the renewal of our minds as the Holy Spirit replaces our self-concept with His Christ concept. This Christ concept asserts that we are a new creation, a restored person possessing a transformed heart, a renewed mind, and a new spirit. We are complete in our union with Jesus Christ. He validates us as He asserts in both word and deed that we are lovable, significant, and secure. We no longer have to seek, for we have been found. We have been given an identity replete with a profound understanding of who we are and what we are to be doing. Therefore, grace now empowers our souls to live out our salvation to our full potential, for it is indeed God who is at work in us both to will and to do of His good pleasure. "Work hard to show the results of your salvation, obeying God with deep reverence and fear. For God is working in you, giving you the desire and the power to do what pleases him" (Phil. 2:12–13).

When we choose to place Christ in His rightful position in our lives, peace and joy begin to pervade as the resident norm. Life now is a continuous process of experiencing Jesus relevantly to our lives—exploring how He is relevant to every new challenge of our souls. We find ourselves compelled to share with each struggling person that which we have found: Jesus loves you, and that makes the difference. This testimony is now the proclamation of a grateful heart that has been touched by the healing love of Jesus Christ. Some may argue with what you believe to be true, but only a fool would seek to criticize the truth you have experienced. Your peace and joy are the proof of a changed life.

However, there is a carnal obstacle to be removed: an individual will not accept validation from a source he or she does not value. Many individuals are not willing to be fulfilled by Jesus' love and be satisfied with Him personally, simply because they do not value Him. They would rather possess the sensual pleasures produced by this world than to experience spiritual intimacy with Jesus Christ. "O Jerusalem, Jerusalem, the city that kills the prophets and stones God's messengers! How often I have wanted to gather your children together as a hen protects her chicks beneath her wings, but you wouldn't let me" (Matt. 23:37).

Where Am I Going?

When we allow God to occupy His designated place in our lives, we can experience a precious rest of sweet harmony. Although we must navigate the maze of earthly living, our minds live in the amazement of heavenly dwelling, for we are experiencing what He desires for us. Though here, we live there. "Since you have been raised to new life with Christ, set your sights on the realities of heaven, where Christ sits in the place of honor at God's right hand. Think about the things of heaven, not the things of earth. For you died to this life, and your real life is hidden with Christ in God" (Col. 3:1–3). We join the ranks of the walking dead, as dead to things earthly but very alive to things heavenly. Carnal potential is given up for spiritual promise. We now see our lives as belonging to Jesus exclusively.

"Then Jesus turned to the Twelve and asked, 'Are you also going to leave?'

"Simon Peter replied, 'Lord, to whom would we go? You have the words that give eternal life'" (John 6:67–68).

"And so, Lord, where do I put my hope? / My only hope is in you" (Ps. 39:7).

Recognizing Christ as our only source of abundant living establishes a desperate dependency on Him. He alone supplies unlimited love, because He is love. Nothing can offer greater significance than the identity as a child of God. No other position is more secure than in God's care, where He states, "Do not be afraid or discouraged, for the Lord will personally go ahead of you. He will be with you; he will neither fail you nor abandon you" (Deut. 31:8). Living with divine enablement for personal empowerment attains ultimate fulfillment. "Dear children, keep away from anything that might take God's place in your hearts" (1 John 5:21). "That's the whole story. Here now is my final conclusion: Fear God and obey his commands, for this is everyone's duty" (Eccles. 12:13).

"For the Kingdom of God is not just a lot of talk; it is living by God's power" (1 Cor. 4:20).

Insight Journal

1. Who am I?
2. I am lovable because:
3. Where am I going?
4. What might take God's place in my heart (1 John 5:21)?
5. Will I choose to be desperately dependent on God?

Psalms Prayer Pattern

Praise the LORD!

I will thank the LORD with all my heart
    as I meet with his godly people.
How amazing are the deeds of the LORD!
    All who delight in him should ponder them.
Everything he does reveals his glory and majesty.
    His righteousness never fails.
He causes us to remember his wonderful works.
    How gracious and merciful is our LORD!
He gives food to those who fear him;
    he always remembers his covenant.
He has shown his great power to his people
    by giving them the lands of other nations.
All he does is just and good,
    and all his commandments are trustworthy.
They are forever true,
    to be obeyed faithfully and with integrity.
He has paid a full ransom for his people.
    He has guaranteed his covenant with them forever.
    What a holy, awe-inspiring name he has!
Fear of the LORD is the foundation of true wisdom.
    All who obey his commandments will grow in wisdom.

Praise him forever!

—Ps. 111

CHAPTER 13

A Job for Job

G OD ASSIGNED JOB the job of demonstrating desperate dependency amid plenty and loss. Our lives are driven by the desire to be successful, and many viewed the life of Job as being a grand success with his ten children, leadership positions, and vast possessions. But when Job was stripped of the people, positions, and possessions, his friends and neighbors would have been hard pressed to label him as a success while he sat on the ash heap mourning his unspeakable losses. However, God does not define success in the same manner we perceive it. "The LORD doesn't see things the way you see them. People judge by outward appearance, but the LORD looks at the heart" (1 Sam. 16:7). God's definition of success is submitting faithfully to His plan for the purpose of glorifying God. In the books of Kings and Chronicles, each king is evaluated on the basis of his commitment to God. Either "he did what was pleasing in the LORD's sight," or "he did what was evil in the LORD's sight." Job's success stemmed from his commitment and willingness to unreservedly submit to the Lord.

The Lord Gives

There once was a man named Job who lived in the land of Uz. He was blameless—a man of complete integrity. He feared God and stayed away from evil. He had seven sons and three daughters. He owned 7,000 sheep, 3,000 camels, 500 teams of oxen, and 500 female donkeys. He also had many servants. He was, in fact, the richest person in that entire area.

Job's sons would take turns preparing feasts in their homes, and they would also invite their three sisters to celebrate with them. When these celebrations ended—sometimes after several days—Job would purify his children. He would get up early in the morning and offer a burnt offering for each of them. For Job said to himself, "Perhaps my children have sinned and have cursed God in their hearts." This was Job's regular practice.

—Job 1:1–5

As we are introduced to Job, he is characterized as a man who exhibited a relevant relationship with God. Submitting faithfully to God, he lived consumed by his connection to God. Every facet of his existence and the concerns of his heart evidenced a dependency on Elohim and an authentic desire to please Him. The community recognized Job as a man who was blameless, full of integrity, and one who feared God and stayed away from evil.

God was intricately involved in Job's life because Job invited God into his life. Although we may not readily embrace this truth, when we invite Christ into our lives it is for better or for worse. The invitation for God to become part of our lives grants Him permission to transform our sinfulness into godliness through whatever means He deems necessary. God's divine enabling shaped Job's identity, molding a lifestyle that had a profound influence upon his society and moved people to take note of God.

Because God was central in Job's life, Job also cared about the relationship his children had with God. As a natural outgrowth of his passion, Job wanted his children to possess what was most important to him—a relationship with Elohim. He did not build his life around his kids, but he endeavored to build his children's lives around God. Party conversations most assuredly remembered "Dad sure will work hard tomorrow to intercede with God on our behalf!" They significantly encountered God through their father's influence.

The process of relating to God became natural because a relationship with God was essential to Job. Reverence for God infiltrated every aspect of his being, polarizing him from his pagan culture, and prioritizing his existence into the image of God. Desperate to be dependent on the One he most revered, the defining aspect of Job's connection was fear that exhibited awe for the One who sustained him. Job's emotional makeup reflected his spiritual connection. He was not anxious about life because he lived in fear of his Lord.

More than religiously acquainted with God, Job was relationally involved with Him. God altered Job's moods. God commanded Job's interests. God occupied Job's thoughts. Job's heart sought God. Job's soul reverenced God. And God was worshiped by Job's being. All Job came to be was shaped by his relational connection to God. Hence, Job was reported by God to be unlike anyone else on the earth. "Then the LORD asked Satan, 'Have you noticed my servant Job? He is the finest man in all the earth. He is blameless—a man of complete integrity. He fears God and stays away from evil'" (1:8). Proudly, Father God bragged on his boy. Such a relationship could never have been casually contrived, but rather nurtured and developed by profound experience based in a deep connection of trust and dependency.

Can Father God brag about you? God loves you because you are His creation. But can He brag on you because you are His elation? You may say you know God loves you, but how do you conduct your life differently because you know God loves you? Do you express your love for Him through gratitude? God loves you so much He has a well-orchestrated plan designed for your life so that you will come into a closer relationship with Him and glorify Him. But are you unreservedly willing to allow Him to accomplish His plan in your life even if it means there would be a book written about your tragic life?

Satan acknowledged a blessed estate existing between God and Job. God knew Job possessed an authentic, trusting relationship, but Satan was not convinced. "Satan replied to the LORD, 'Yes, but Job has good reason to fear God. You have always put a wall of protection around him and his home and his property. You have made him prosper in everything he does. Look how rich he is! But reach out and take away everything he has, and he will surely curse you to your face!'" (1:9–11).

The Lord Takes Away

"All right, you may test him," the LORD said to Satan. "Do whatever you want with everything he possesses, but don't harm him physically." So Satan left the LORD's presence.

One day when Job's sons and daughters were feasting at the oldest brother's house, a messenger arrived at Job's home with this news: "Your oxen were plowing, with the donkeys feeding beside them, when the Sabeans raided us. They stole all the animals and killed all the farmhands. I am the only one who escaped to tell you."

While he was still speaking, another messenger arrived with this news: "The fire of God has fallen from heaven and burned up your sheep and all the shepherds. I am the only one who escaped to tell you."

While he was still speaking, a third messenger arrived with this news: "Three bands of Chaldean raiders have stolen your camels and killed your servants. I am the only one who escaped to tell you."

While he was still speaking, another messenger arrived with this news: "Your sons and daughters were feasting in their oldest brother's home. Suddenly, a powerful wind swept in from the wilderness and hit the house on all sides. The house collapsed, and all your children are dead. I am the only one who escaped to tell you."

—Job 1:12–19

At this point in the story, every fiber of our being stands in judgment against God, casting dispersion on His name. "If You love me, why would You allow this to happen?" Hardly can God be understood while being weighed in the balance of our pain. Yet, God in His love uses suffering as a platform to convey the depths of His sovereignty. God will save us. God will sustain us. God will promote our best interest. But His ways are beyond our comprehension. It is through suffering that we learn to rely on Him. Our trials become an example of the sufficiency of Christ. The beauty of His heart becomes the bounty of our lives as we encounter Him and His faithfulness.

It is in this vein that God uses Job as tangible evidence to illustrate the truth about Himself. In the depths of despair God develops in us the capacity to live beyond ourselves through His grace, which, practically understood, is the power to live supplied by God. Job's dire situation produced desperate dependency upon God and facilitated communion with God in response to his loss and suffering. Job had already given everything to God, so it was not without his permission that God followed through to use Job as He desired.

Job stood up and tore his robe in grief. Then he shaved his head and fell to the ground to worship. He said,

"I came naked from my mother's womb,
    and I will be naked when I leave.
The Lord gave me what I had,
    and the Lord has taken it away.
Praise the name of the Lord!"

In all of this, Job did not sin by blaming God.

—Job 1:20–22

Job assumed God's sovereign involvement in the course of life that he could not control. In Job's mind God's presence was not only acknowledged in his suffering, but His will was ascribed to it. In response to his bereavement, Job asserted a benediction of blessing to the Lord. In the midst of his tragedy, Job worshipped while submitting to God's sovereign right to rule over his person, positions, and possessions.

Even though Job suffered tremendous loss, Father God could still brag on His boy again.

> Then the LORD asked Satan, "Have you noticed my servant Job? He is the finest man in all the earth. He is blameless—a man of complete integrity. He fears God and stays away from evil. And he has maintained his integrity, even though you urged me to harm him without cause."
>
> Satan replied to the LORD, "Skin for skin! A man will give up everything he has to save his life. But reach out and take away his health, and he will surely curse you to your face!"
>
> "All right, do with him as you please," the LORD said to Satan. "But spare his life." So Satan left the LORD's presence, and he struck Job with terrible boils from head to foot.
>
> Job scraped his skin with a piece of broken pottery as he sat among the ashes. His wife said to him, "Are you still trying to maintain your integrity? Curse God and die."
>
> But Job replied, "You talk like a foolish woman. Should we accept only good things from the hand of God and never anything bad?" So in all this, Job said nothing wrong.
>
> —Job 2:3–10

The moral character of God held Job constant even though his mortal condition was completely in chaos. Overwhelmed by his limitations, he could only find comfort in total self-abandonment through trust. Delimited by his dependency, Job had no other choice but to interpret the nature of his anguish through the moral attributes of a holy, righteous, just, and good God who is full of truth. All of Job's philosophical ponderings, including his frustration and confusion, were delineated by his dependence on God, making him more desperate than ever. In Job's agony his dilemma was to understand life's new normal consistently with the truth about God.

Unaided by mortals, Job found comfort in the truth of God and confessed that he had not denied God's truth. "At least I can take comfort in this: / Despite the pain, / I have not denied the words of the Holy One" (6:10).

Contrary to popular belief, God's plans may include, "I, too, have been assigned months of futility, / long and weary nights of misery" (7:3). But tormented by turmoil, Job labored to understand God and his position with God.

> "What are people, that you should make so much of us,
>   that you should think of us so often?
> For you examine us every morning
>   and test us every moment.
> Why won't you leave me alone,
>   at least long enough for me to swallow!
> If I have sinned, what have I done to you,
>   O watcher of all humanity?
> Why make me your target?
>   Am I a burden to you?
> Why not just forgive my sin
>   and take away my guilt?
> For soon I will lie down in the dust and die.
>   When you look for me, I will be gone."
>
> —Job 7:17–21

With no one else to turn to, Job's suffering launched him into uncharted territory as he encountered God. For better or worse, Job saw God as his only course of action. His previous experiences with God had not educated Job to the nature of this encounter. Hence Job cried out to God, seeking to reconcile this version of life with what he did not understand about God.

Within his confusion and frustration, Job's humility prompted a deeper connection with God through contemplation. In this contemplation he considered God's unfathomable essence and righteousness: "Yes, I know all this is true in principle. / But how can a person be declared innocent in God's sight? / If someone wanted to take God to court, / would it be possible to answer him even once in a thousand times? / For God is so wise and so mighty. / Who has ever challenged him successfully?" (9:2–4).

Frightened by God's rule of supremacy and thwarted by His transcendence, Job recognized he could not manipulate God. "So who am I, that I should try to answer God / or even reason with him? / Even if I were right, I would have no defense. / I could only plead for mercy. / And even if I summoned him and he responded, / I'm not sure he would listen to me" (9:14–16). Through deeper humility came deeper dependency.

None of the greatest human defense mechanisms—including pretense, denial, or disassociation—would work to manage the depths of Job's suffering. Left with the honest reality of his great torment and the actuality of the anguish he could not escape, he protested his predicament: "I am disgusted with my life. / Let me complain freely. / My bitter soul must complain" (10:1).

Dialoging with God establishes a foundation where healing can begin. Job chose to communicate with the language of complaint to connect his wounded soul to his Sustainer. He was not condemned for relating in honesty and truth with purity. Persistent in trust, though faced with temptation to mutiny against his Lord and his own disquieted soul, Job postured to magnify God even though in the language of complaint. His desire was not to be insubordinate. He came with an attitude of a soul prostrate before God, searching for the ability to trust. Even amid his paradigm of dependency, the crisis moved him beyond his maturity: "I will say to God, 'Don't simply condemn me— / tell me the charge you are bringing against me'" (10:2).

Because of Job's intimate relationship with God, he desired to know the heart of God. Throughout his ordeal he maintained his trust that God also desired a relationship with him. Believing this, Job was convinced that if he had done something wrong God would reveal it to him so a close connection could be maintained. "Yet my friends laugh at me, / for I call on God and expect an answer. / I am a just and blameless man, / yet they laugh at me" (12:4).

Disorientated, Job was unable to walk away, but he also found it intolerable to stay bound by the shackles of suffering and pain as he loathed even his next breath. Yet he clung to God desperately, as one fearful of losing his grasp upon Him. Job knew that comprehending the nature of his suffering ultimately was beyond the range of his human ability. How could a mere man understand that which is from God's hand?

"But true wisdom and power are found in God; / counsel and understanding are his" (12:13).

More than just an experience with suffering, God was perfecting Job's relationship with Him. In the kiln of trials we must yield as God conforms us into the image of His Son. It is in the dark places that the metal of a relationship is hammered into the form God desires it to be. Crisis ignited the flame, which provided the necessary heat to forge Job into deeper desperate dependency on God. Suffering draped the backdrop and created the context and the impetus through which purification could occur. God views our limitations not in terms of how much we can withstand, but in terms of what will it take to bring His children closer to Him and produce simultaneously His likeness within us.

You may ask, "How do I interpret suffering, that which is typically viewed as evil, in the light of an all-powerful God who is sovereign?" Without understanding how everything fit in the construct of his life, Job depended on the truth that God is good. This allowed Job to cry out to God in reverent fear with the hope of receiving mercy. How does this suffering coincide with the goodness of God? Job's line of questioning did not doubt God's moral character, but was in deference to His moral character: "Why are these things happening in light of who You are?"

Job's striving was to understand how to live with God's plan.

"Be silent now and leave me alone.
    Let me speak, and I will face the consequences.
Yes, I will take my life in my hands
    and say what I really think.
God might kill me, but I have no other hope.
    I am going to argue my case with him.
But this is what will save me—I am not godless.
    If I were, I could not stand before him."

—Job 13:13–16

Plagued with pain and persecuted by false accusations, Job's plight was amplified by well-meaning comforters who did not understand the ways of God and could not discern the will of God in Job's life. It is an awesome responsibility to attempt to speak for God. Unfortunately, these friends did not have an intimate relationship with God that enabled them to accurately relay God's messages to Job. Those who assumed they comprehended God robbed Job of consolation: "I have heard all this before. / What miserable comforters you are!" (16:2). Disappointed by his miserable comforters, Job sought the face of God more desperately: "My friends scorn me, / but I pour out my tears to God" (16:20).

While Job's counselors judged him according to circumstances, Job judged himself according to God's Word. His integrity was not based in his own subjective belief that he was good, but he held tightly to his faith in Elohim's provision of atoning forgiveness,

His process of providing holiness, and His persistent caring connection. Amid accusation, opposition, and suffering, Job rendered judgment on his friends based also on the words of God's truth. In Job's mind, only God could be right.

Still I Will Trust Him

In the midst of his complaint Job came to clarity. What God has willed cannot be overruled by reasoning. Rather, what God has determined must be trusted. Job had no other rational option than to desperately depend upon the reality that the arms of God holding him with loving embrace surrounded his pain and anguish. With prophetic enlightenment Job tenaciously affirmed,

"Oh, that my words could be recorded.
     Oh, that they could be inscribed on a monument,
carved with an iron chisel and filled with lead,
     engraved forever in the rock.

"But as for me, I know that my Redeemer lives,
     and he will stand upon the earth at last.
And after my body has decayed,
     yet in my body I will see God!
I will see him for myself.
     Yes, I will see him with my own eyes.
     I am overwhelmed at the thought!"

—Job 19:23–27

Although his crisis was still unresolved, Job clung to the faithful justice of God.

"My complaint today is still a bitter one,
     and I try hard not to groan aloud.
If only I knew where to find God,
     I would go to his court.
I would lay out my case
     and present my arguments.
Then I would listen to his reply
     and understand what he says to me.

Would he use his great power to argue with me?
No, he would give me a fair hearing.
Honest people can reason with him,
so I would be forever acquitted by my judge."

—Job 23:2–7

Unable to sense, experience, or discern the presence of God in the midst of his calamity, Job was confident God had not lost him and certain that at the completion of God's plan Job would be purified. "But he knows where I am going. / And when he tests me, I will come out as pure as gold" (23:10). The best choice is to trust Him. "But once he has made his decision, who can change his mind? / Whatever he wants to do, he does. / So he will do to me whatever he has planned. He controls my destiny" (23:13–14).

Thwarted by lack of experience, Job could not find God relevant to his crisis. Never before had these men been exposed to the suffering of the righteous. They had to contend with how to reconcile tragedy with their limited understanding of God. The missing pieces prevented them from conceiving that calamity could befall the godly.

Then the LORD answered Job from the whirlwind:

"Who is this that questions my wisdom
with such ignorant words?
Brace yourself like a man,
because I have some questions for you,
and you must answer them."

—Job 38:1–3

Before God could enlighten these men to a greater knowledge of who He is, He first had to remind them of who they were. So God answered Job from a whirlwind to produce the trauma of truth. God's voice coming from a whirlwind certainly was disconcerting enough, but then came the barrage of unanswerable questions. Brokenness followed.

Then Job replied to the Lord,

"I am nothing—how could I ever find the answers?
    I will cover my mouth with my hand.
I have said too much already.
    I have nothing more to say."

—Job 40:3–5

Obviously God is the only one who can answer all questions, but He is not obligated to do so. Sunday school teacher Steve Swafford stated, "Life is too complicated for simple answers." Only God can adequately deal with the answers to all questions. We must succumb to trusting Him. He always knows best.

Then Job replied to the Lord:

"I know that you can do anything,
    and no one can stop you.
You asked, 'Who is this that questions my wisdom with such ignorance?'
    It is I—and I was talking about things I knew nothing about,
    things far too wonderful for me.
You said, 'Listen and I will speak!
    I have some questions for you,
    and you must answer them.'
I had only heard about you before,
    but now I have seen you with my own eyes.
I take back everything I said,
    and I sit in dust and ashes to show my repentance."

—Job 42:1–6

After a fresh encounter with God and His sovereignty, Job could see with new eyes the awesomeness of God. God is relevant to every area of life because He alone "causes everything to work together for the good of those who love God and are called according to his purpose for them" (Rom. 8:28). Instead of striving to understand why, we should endeavor to know who God is. As we grow in our knowledge of Him we can move more easily past the barriers that obstruct a trusting relationship.

"And you will know the truth, and the truth will set you free" (John 8:32).

Perhaps we are pawns on the chessboard of the Master, but we can choose to be participants and be confident that He has placed us as part of His strategic plan. Our sovereign God designates each person's position—some to be kings, some to be queens, others to be bishops, knights, and pawns. But we are all mere servants of our great God and stewards of the ministry of Jesus Christ. In God's government, even kings are pawns. He sets them up and takes them down to accomplish His purposes. God can do whatever He wants and, yes, we are supposed to be OK with that.

Are you willing to live for the glory of God? Many will equate this question with achieving excellence. Yes, they proclaim, I will be successful for His glory. However, God's definition of success is submitting faithfully to God's plan for the purpose of glorifying Him. God created and designed you so He could be in a relationship with you. Everything that happens is for the purpose of leading you into a deeper relationship with Him. Are you ready for that kind of adventure?

Insight Journal

1. How does God fit into the picture of my life?
2. I realized I could not live life successfully by myself when ...
3. What have I believed about God that I now know is not true? How did learning the truth about God change me?
4. What truths have I clung to tightly even when others did not agree? What are the Scripture references that validate these as truths?
5. Will I submit to God so He can achieve His purpose in my life? What do I need to submit to God so He can receive glory?

Psalms Prayer Pattern

O God, you are my God;
    I earnestly search for you.
My soul thirsts for you;
    my whole body longs for you
in this parched and weary land
    where there is no water.
I have seen you in your sanctuary
    and gazed upon your power and glory.
Your unfailing love is better than life itself;
    how I praise you!
I will praise you as long as I live,
    lifting up my hands to you in prayer.
You satisfy me more than the richest feast.
    I will praise you with songs of joy.

I lie awake thinking of you,
    meditating on you through the night.
Because you are my helper,
    I sing for joy in the shadow of your wings.
I cling to you;
    your strong right hand holds me securely.

But those plotting to destroy me will come to ruin.
    They will go down into the depths of the earth.
They will die by the sword
    and become the food of jackals.
But the king will rejoice in God.
    All who trust in him will praise him,
    while liars will be silenced.

—Ps. 63

Epilogue

WE TOOK OVER a year to process *Desperate Dependency* with our small group of forty singles. Together we waded through deep waters of much hurt and pain as we struggled to find Christ relevant to daily living and a myriad of crises. As we looked through the magnifying glass of each other's lives, we continuously asked, How is God relevant to this area of life? How will God receive glory from this issue? How will He be central instead of me being central?

The constant struggle is to die to our desires so that we might glorify God instead. Joel acknowledged the constant dilemma: "I've got life and all my issues, and I magnify that." But the ultimate happiness in our lives is for God to get glory through our lives.

Do we trust God to redeem us from the evil that has touched our lives? Kauri noted that desperate dependency is not just about lying on the floor helpless in the fetal position, saying, "I can't do this." But going past that, saying, "No matter how difficult this is, I want God to be glorified through my life." "Yay, God!" God can be glorified no matter what! If one is born blind, God can be glorified (John 9:1–3). Even if we have chosen sin, God can still be glorified in our lives. We must be motivated to see how Christ is relevant to every situation. "OK, Jesus, how are You going to make a difference here?"

We also challenged each other to not forget Christ is relevant in the joys and successes. If we do not see Christ as relevant in the good times, we will become prideful and self-sufficient and move back toward independence. Dependency is the only option for authentic Christian living.

No one in our small group, including Kirk and me, would say we have successfully arrived at the destination of desperate dependency and finding Christ relevant to every area of life. But we have grown in our awareness of His working in our lives to bring us to godliness, and we are striving to allow Christ's redemptive process to function in our lives instead of self's redemptive process.

> I trust that my life will bring honor to Christ, whether I live or die. For to me, living means living for Christ, and dying is even better. But if I live, I can do more fruitful work for Christ. So I really don't know which is better. I'm torn between two desires: I long to go and be with Christ, which would be far better for me. But for your sakes, it is better that I continue to live.
>
> Knowing this, I am convinced that I will remain alive so I can continue to help all of you grow and experience the joy of your faith. And when I come to you again, you will have even more reason to take pride in Christ Jesus because of what he is doing through me.
>
> —Phil. 1:20–26

"So we keep on praying for you, asking our God to enable you to live a life worthy of his call. May he give you the power to accomplish all the good things your faith prompts you to do" (2 Thess. 1:11).

Fruit Chart

S O I SAY, let the Holy Spirit guide your lives. Then you won't be doing what your sinful nature craves. The sinful nature wants to do evil, which is just the opposite of what the Spirit wants. And the Spirit gives us desires that are the opposite of what the sinful nature desires. These two forces are constantly fighting each other, so you are not free to carry out your good intentions. But when you are directed by the Spirit, you are not under obligation to the law of Moses.

When you follow the desires of your sinful nature, the results are very clear: sexual immorality, impurity, lustful pleasures, idolatry, sorcery, hostility, quarreling, jealousy, outbursts of anger, selfish ambition, dissension, division, envy, drunkenness, wild parties, and other sins like these. Let me tell you again, as I have before, that anyone living that sort of life will not inherit the Kingdom of God.

But the Holy Spirit produces this kind of fruit in our lives: love, joy, peace, patience, kindness, goodness, faithfulness, gentleness, and self-control. There is no law against these things!

Those who belong to Christ Jesus have nailed the passions and desires of their sinful nature to his cross and crucified them there. Since we are living by the Spirit, let us follow the Spirit's leading in every part of our lives" (Gal. 5:16–25).

FRUIT OF SPIRIT	EVIDENCE OF FRUIT	COUNTERFEIT	CULMINATION
LOVE	VALUE OTHERS	self-centeredness	*emptiness*
JOY	RELIANCE ON GOD	pleasure	*futility*
PEACE	SECURITY IN CHRIST	comfort	*turmoil*
PATIENCE	PERSEVERE BY SPIRIT	control	*frustration*
KINDNESS	SHOW GOD'S LOVE	manipulation	*anger*
GOODNESS	EXEMPLIFY CHRIST	exploitation	*inadequacy*
FAITHFULNESS	TRUST CHRIST	pretense	*anxiety*
GENTLENESS	REFLECT GOD'S GRACE	selfish ambition	*alienation*
SELF-CONTROL	SUBMIT TO SPIRIT	self-indulgence	*discouragement*

ACTION VERSE

Dear friends, let us continue to love one another, for love comes from God. Anyone who loves is a child of God and knows God. But anyone who does not love does not know God, for God is love. (1 John 4:7–8)

I pray that God, the source of hope, will fill you completely with joy and peace because you trust in him. Then you will overflow with confident hope through the power of the Holy Spirit. (Rom. 15:13)

Don't worry about anything; instead, pray about everything. Tell God what you need, and thank him for all he has done. Then you will experience God's peace, which exceeds anything we can understand. His peace will guard your hearts and minds as you live in Christ Jesus. (Phil. 4:6–7)

Always be humble and gentle. Be patient with each other, making allowance for each other's faults because of your love. Make every effort to keep yourselves united in the Spirit, binding yourselves together with peace. (Eph. 4:2–3)

Since God chose you to be the holy people he loves, you must clothe yourselves with tenderhearted mercy, kindness, humility, gentleness, and patience. (Col. 3:12)

Don't be selfish; don't try to impress others. Be humble, thinking of others as better than yourselves. Don't look out only for your own interests, but take an interest in others, too. (Phil. 2:3–4)

And it is impossible to please God without faith. Anyone who wants to come to him must believe that God exists and that he rewards those who sincerely seek him. (Heb. 11:6)

Gently instruct those who oppose the truth. Perhaps God will change those people's hearts, and they will learn the truth. (2 Tim. 2:25)

Those who are dominated by the sinful nature think about sinful things, but those who are controlled by the Holy Spirit think about things that please the Spirit. So letting your sinful nature control your mind leads to death. But letting the Spirit control your mind leads to life and peace. (Rom. 8:5–6)

The Blessed Man

I N CHAPTER 4 we pointed out that the ultimate reality is that God did not design happiness as our life's goal. God designed us to be in an intimate relationship with Him, with happiness being the result of our union with Him. Therefore, all of our endeavors should be fostering our connection to Him as we conform to His image. So what do the Scriptures say about how to connect with God that results in becoming a "blessed man"?

Connect to God's Word

> *Oh, the joys of those who do not*
> > *follow the advice of the wicked,*
> > *or stand around with sinners,*
> > *or join in with mockers.* (Ps. 1:1)

> *Joyful are people of integrity,*
> > *who follow the instructions of the LORD.*
> *Joyful are those who obey his laws*
> > *and search for him with all their hearts.* (Ps. 119:1–2)

> *"And so, my children, listen to me,*
> > *for all who follow my ways are joyful.*
> *Listen to my instruction and be wise.*
> > *Don't ignore it.*

> Joyful are those who listen to me,
>> watching for me daily at my gates,
>> waiting for me outside my home!
> For whoever finds me finds life
>> and receives favor from the LORD." (Prov. 8:32–35)

❧ Then when they were alone, he turned to the disciples and said, "Blessed are the eyes that see what you have seen." (Luke 10:23)

❧ As Jesus was saying these things, a woman in the crowd called out, "Blessed is the mother who gave you birth and nursed you."

He replied, "Blessed rather are those who hear the word of God and obey it." (Luke 11:27–28 NIV)

❧ "Now that you know these things, you will be blessed if you do them." (John 13:17 NIV)

❧ Blessed is the one who reads the words of this prophecy, and blessed are those who hear it and take to heart what is written in it, because the time is near. (Rev. 1:3 NIV)

❧ "Look, I am coming soon! Blessed are those who obey the words of prophecy written in this book." (Rev. 22:7)

Trust God

❧ Blessed is the man
>> who makes the LORD his trust,
> who does not look to the proud,
>> to those who turn aside to false gods. (Ps. 40:4 NIV)

❧ O LORD Almighty,
>> blessed is the man who trusts in you. (Ps. 84:12 NIV)

❧ "But blessed is the man who trusts in the LORD,
>> whose confidence is in him." (Jer. 17:7 NIV)

❧ Yet the LORD longs to be gracious to you;
>> he rises to show you compassion.
> For the LORD is a God of justice.
>> Blessed are all who wait for him! (Isa. 30:18 NIV)

❧ Then Jesus told him, "Because you have seen me, you have believed; blessed are those who have not seen and yet have believed." (John 20:29 NIV)

Experience Forgiveness of Sin

❧ *Oh, what joy for those*
  whose disobedience is forgiven,
  whose sin is put out of sight!
Yes, what joy for those
  whose record the Lord *has cleared of guilt,*
  whose lives are lived in complete honesty! (Ps. 32:1–2)

❧ *"Blessed are they*
  whose transgressions are forgiven,
  whose sins are covered.
Blessed is the man
  whose sin the Lord will never count against him." (Rom. 4:7–8 NIV)

Desire Righteousness

❧ *Blessed are they who maintain justice,*
  who constantly do what is right. (Ps. 106:3 NIV)

❧ *This is what the* Lord *says:*
"Be just and fair to all.
  Do what is right and good,
for I am coming soon to rescue you
  and to display my righteousness among you.
Blessed are all those
  who are careful to do this." (Isa. 56:1–2a)

❧ *"Blessed are those who hunger and thirst for righteousness,*
  for they shall be satisfied." (Matt. 5:6 NASB)

Fear the Lord

❧ *Blessed is the man who fears the* Lord,
  who finds great delight in his commands. (Ps. 112:1b NIV)

❧ *How blessed is everyone who fears the* Lord,
Who walks in His ways.

When you shall eat of the fruit of your hands,
You will be happy and it will be well with you. (Ps. 128:1–2 NASB)

Find Strength in God

ॐ *Blessed are those whose strength is in you,*
who have set their hearts on pilgrimage. (Ps. 84:5 NIV)

Take Refuge in God

ॐ *Submit to God's royal son, or he will become angry,*
and you will be destroyed in the midst of all your activities—
for his anger flares up in an instant.
But what joy for all who take refuge in him! (Ps. 2:12)

ॐ *Taste and see that the LORD is good;*
blessed is the man who takes refuge in him. (Ps. 34:8 NIV)

Rest

ॐ *"Blessed are those who honor my Sabbath days of rest*
and keep themselves from doing wrong." (Isa. 56:2b)

Don't Be Offended by God

ॐ *"And tell him, 'God blesses those who do not turn away because of me.'"* (Matt. 11:6)

ॐ *"Blessed is the man who does not fall away on account of me."* (Luke 7:23 NIV)

Accept Discipline

ॐ *Joyful are those you discipline, LORD,*
those you teach with your instructions. (Ps. 94:12)

Realize Your Need

ॐ *"Blessed are the poor in spirit,*
for theirs is the kingdom of heaven." (Matt. 5:3 NIV)

ⵣ *Then Jesus turned to his disciples and said,*
    "God blesses you who are poor,
        for the Kingdom of God is yours." (Luke 6:20)

Mourn

ⵣ *"God blesses those who mourn,*
    for they will be comforted." (Matt. 5:4)

ⵣ *"Blessed are you who hunger now,*
    for you will be satisfied.
Blessed are you who weep now,
    for you will laugh." (Luke 6:21 NIV)

Be Humble

ⵣ *"Blessed are the meek,*
    for they will inherit the earth." (Matt. 5:5 NIV)

Be Pure in Heart

ⵣ *"Blessed are the pure in heart,*
    for they will see God." (Matt. 5:8 NIV)

Be a Peacemaker

ⵣ *"Blessed are the peacemakers,*
    for they will be called sons of God." (Matt. 5:9 NIV)

Encounter Persecution

ⵣ *"Blessed are those who are persecuted because of righteousness,*
    for theirs is the kingdom of heaven.
"Blessed are you when people insult you, persecute you and falsely say all kinds of evil against you because of me." (Matt. 5:10–11 NIV)

ⵣ *"Blessed are you when men hate you,*
    when they exclude you and insult you

> *and reject your name as evil,*
> *because of the Son of Man." (Luke 6:22 NIV)*

∅ *But even if you should suffer for what is right, you are blessed. "Do not fear what they fear; do not be frightened." (1 Peter 3:14 NIV)*

∅ *So be happy when you are insulted for being a Christian, for then the glorious Spirit of God rests upon you. (1 Peter 4:14)*

Endure Temptation

∅ *Blessed is the man who perseveres under trial, because when he has stood the test, he will receive the crown of life that God has promised to those who love him. (James 1:12 NIV)*

Consider the Less Fortunate

∅ *How blessed is he who considers the helpless;*
The Lord will deliver him in a day of trouble. (Ps. 41:1 NASB)

∅ *"But when you give a banquet, invite the poor, the crippled, the lame, the blind, and you will be blessed. Although they cannot repay you, you will be repaid at the resurrection of the righteous." (Luke 14:13–14 NIV)*

Enjoy Worship

∅ *Blessed are those who have learned to acclaim you,*
who walk in the light of your presence, O Lord. (Ps. 89:15 NIV)

Live with God

∅ *Blessed are those who dwell in your house;*
they are ever praising you. (Ps. 84:4 NIV)

∅ *And the angel said to me, "Write this: Blessed are those who are invited to the wedding feast of the Lamb." And he added, "These are true words that come from God." (Rev. 19:9)*

Die in the Lord

🎵 *And I heard a voice from heaven saying, "Write this down: Blessed are those who die in the Lord from now on. Yes, says the Spirit, they are blessed indeed, for they will rest from their hard work; for their good deeds follow them!"* (Rev. 14:13)

Do Your Part

🎵 *"Blessed is that servant whom his master, when he comes, will find so doing."* (Matt. 24:46 NKJV)

🎵 *"Blessed are those servants whom the master, when he comes, will find watching. Assuredly, I say to you that he will gird himself and have them sit down to eat, and will come and serve them."* (Luke 12:37 NKJV)

🎵 *"Blessed is that slave whom his master finds so doing when he comes."* (Luke 12:43 NASB)

🎵 *"Behold, I come like a thief! Blessed is he who stays awake and keeps his clothes with him, so that he may not go naked and be shamefully exposed."* (Rev. 16:15 NIV)

🎵 *Blessed are those who wash their robes. They will be permitted to enter through the gates of the city and eat the fruit from the tree of life.* (Rev. 22:14)

Bad Belief/Good God

WHILE COMPLETING THE Insight Journal of chapter 5 you asked yourself, "Based on my behavior, what do I believe about God?" Perhaps you reluctantly admitted you possessed a bad belief. If you could not identify your bad belief, use this chart to stimulate your thinking to determine what deceptions keep you in bondage.

In chapter 12 we addressed the significance of names in Scripture. God provides an extensive list of names whereby we can come to know Him more intimately. These names describe God's person, position, and possessions. Through these identifications we can realize that as His child we have all the resources we need.

By integrating our bad beliefs and the names of our good God, we can recognize that God is fully capable of addressing each of our bad beliefs through His unfathomable character. We need to connect to Him in the ways He has revealed Himself through His names, so His truth can combat our bad beliefs. Every bad belief is a distortion of God's nature and intended by Satan to build a wall between God and us. But when we can identify our bad beliefs and appropriate the Spirit of our good God, the strongholds of Satan will be broken.

May God give you more and more grace and peace as you grow in your knowledge of God and Jesus our Lord.

By his divine power, God has given us everything we need for living a godly life. We have received all of this by coming to know him, the one who called us to himself by means of his marvelous glory and excellence.

—2 Peter 1:2–3

BAD BELIEF	GOOD GOD
God does not love me. God doesn't want a relationship with me.	*Abba* Father (Rom. 8:14-17)
God exists to serve me.	*Adonai* Sovereign Ruler, Master (Ps. 8)
God has set me up for failure.	*Elohim* All Powerful One, Creator (Ps. 68)
God can't be trusted with my well-being.	*El Elyon* The God Most High (Ps. 7)
God won't make that person pay, so I must seek satisfaction.	*El Gmulot* The God of Recompense (Jer. 51:56)
God does not care about me. God does not care about my best interest.	*El Roi* The God Who Sees Me (Ps. 139)
God is not enough.	*El Shaddai* The All Sufficient One, God Almighty (Ps. 91)
I can take care of myself.	*Jehovah* The Self-Existent One (Ps. 102)
God will not provide what I need.	*Jehovah-Jireh* The Lord Will Provide (Gen. 22:9-14)
God will excuse my sin.	*Jehovah-M'Kaddesh* The Lord Who Sanctifies (Lev. 20:7-8)
God should help me get what I want.	*Jehovah-Saboath* The Lord of Hosts (Isa. 6:1-5)
God wants me to hurt. God cannot heal the pain.	*Jehovah-Rapha* The Lord Who Heals (Ps. 103)
I am not worthy for God to love.	*Jehovah-Rohi* The Lord is My Shepherd (Ps. 23)
God has left me alone.	*Jehovah-Shammah* The Lord Is There (1 Cor. 6:19-20)
God does not want me to be happy.	*Jehovah-Shalom* The Lord Our Peace (John 14:27)
God wants me to be happy.	*Jehovah-Tsidkenu* The Lord Our Righteousness (Jer. 23:5-6)

Evaluation of Desperate Dependency

W E HAVE INCLUDED Psalm 119 here as a personal evaluation tool to assist you in determining your status as an individual who is desperately dependent on God. This exercise is not designed to create a monument to your success or failure as a Christian. Rather, allow it to serve as a compass that establishes a "true north" so you may align your path to arrive at the ultimate destination of Christlikeness. The author of this psalm testifies to the paths he has taken along his course of relating to God. Therefore this instrument may also offer guidance for your direction as you attempt to follow the way to godliness.

Warren Wiersbe offers this introduction to Psalm 119:

This psalm is special in several ways. It is the longest psalm (176 verses), and it is an acrostic psalm, following the letters of the Hebrew alphabet. In most editions of the Bible, the twenty-two sections of this psalm are headed by the successive letters of the Hebrew alphabet (Aleph, Beth, Gimel, etc.). In the Hebrew Bible, each verse in a section begins with that Hebrew letter. For example, all the verses in the "aleph" section (vv. 1–8) begin with the Hebrew letter "aleph." Look at the "teth" section (vv. 65–72) and start v. 67 with "Til" and v. 71 with "Tis," and you will have each line starting with the English letter "T" (which is the same as the Hebrew "teth"). The Jews wrote in this fashion to help them memorize the Scriptures so they could meditate on God's Word. We do not know who wrote this psalm, although the writer refers to himself many times. He was suffering for his love for God's Law (vv. 22, 50–53, 95, 98, 115), yet he had determined to obey the

Word regardless of the cost. All but five verses mention the Word of God in one way or another. The exceptions are vv. 84, 90, 121, 122, and 132. God is referred to in every verse....Each section has eight verses....The word "eight" in Hebrew literally means "abundance, more than enough"; it is the number of new beginnings. It is as though the writer is saying, "God's Word is enough. If you have the Scriptures, that is all you need for life and godliness." Indeed the Bible points us to Christ: He is the Living Word about whom the written Word speaks.[1]

As you read through this psalm, mark the verses that *currently* and *consistently* (more often than not) describe you. We have also created a personalization of each verse so that you can more easily determine an accurate assessment. Since Psalm 119 is composed of 176 verses, it may be necessary to complete this review in stages. Take your time, and allow God to use this exercise to draw you closer to Himself.

Psalm 119

Aleph (א)

¹Joyful are people of integrity, / who follow the instructions of the LORD.
- ☐ *I am joyful, have integrity, and follow the instructions of the* LORD.

²Joyful are those who obey his laws / and search for him with all their hearts.
- ☐ *I obey the laws of the* LORD, *am joyful, and search for the* LORD *with all of my heart.*

³They do not compromise with evil, / and they walk only in his paths.
- ☐ *I do not compromise with evil and walk only in the* LORD's *paths.*

⁴You have charged us / to keep your commandments carefully.
- ☐ *I keep the* LORD's *commandments carefully.*

⁵Oh, that my actions would consistently / reflect your decrees!
- ☐ *I wish that my actions would consistently reflect the decrees of the* LORD!

⁶Then I will not be ashamed / when I compare my life with your commands.
- ☐ *I am not ashamed when I compare my life with the commands of the* LORD.

⁷As I learn your righteous regulations, / I will thank you by living as I should!
- ☐ *I learn the righteous regulations of the* LORD *and thank the* LORD *by living as I should.*

⁸I will obey your decrees. / Please don't give up on me!
- ☐ *I obey the decrees of the* LORD.

Beth (ב)

⁹How can a young person stay pure? / By obeying your word.
- ☐ *I stay pure by obeying the word of the Lord.*

¹⁰I have tried hard to find you— / don't let me wander from your commands.
- ☐ *I have tried hard to find the Lord. I desire to follow the Lord's commands.*

¹¹I have hidden your word in my heart, / that I might not sin against you.
- ☐ *I have hidden the word of the Lord in my heart so that I might not sin against Him.*

¹²I praise you, O Lord; / teach me your decrees.
- ☐ *I praise the Lord and desire to learn His decrees.*

¹³I have recited aloud / all the regulations you have given us.
- ☐ *I recite aloud the regulations the Lord has given me.*

¹⁴I have rejoiced in your laws / as much as in riches.
- ☐ *I rejoice in the Lord's laws as much as I would rejoice in being rich.*

¹⁵I will study your commandments / and reflect on your ways.
- ☐ *I study the Lord's commandments and reflect on the ways of the Lord.*

¹⁶I will delight in your decrees / and not forget your word.
- ☐ *I delight in the decrees of the Lord and do not forget the word of the Lord.*

Gimel (ג)

¹⁷Be good to your servant, / that I may live and obey your word.
- ☐ *God enables me to live and obey His word.*

¹⁸Open my eyes to see / the wonderful truths in your instructions.
- ☐ *I ask the Lord to open my eyes to see the wonderful truths in His instructions.*

¹⁹I am only a foreigner in the land. / Don't hide your commands from me!
- ☐ *I feel like I don't belong, so I ask the Lord to reveal His commands to me.*

²⁰I am always overwhelmed / with a desire for your regulations.
- ☐ *I am overwhelmed with a desire for the Lord's regulations.*

²¹You rebuke the arrogant; / those who wander from your commands are cursed.
- ☐ *The Lord disciplines me when I am arrogant or wander from His commands.*

²²Don't let them scorn and insult me, / for I have obeyed your laws.
> ☐ *I ask the Lord to protect me because I obey the laws of the Lord.*

²³Even princes sit and speak against me, / but I will meditate on your decrees.
> ☐ *I meditate on the decrees of the Lord even when others speak against me.*

²⁴Your laws please me; / they give me wise advice.
> ☐ *The laws of the Lord please me and give me wise advice.*

Daleth (ד)

²⁵I lie in the dust; / revive me by your word.
> ☐ *When I feel like I am lying in the dust, the word of the Lord revives me.*

²⁶I told you my plans, and you answered. / Now teach me your decrees.
> ☐ *I told the Lord my plans and He answered me. Now I ask the Lord to teach me His plans.*

²⁷Help me understand the meaning of your commandments, / and I will meditate on your wonderful deeds.
> ☐ *I ask the Lord to help me understand the meaning of His commandments. I meditate on His wonderful deeds.*

²⁸I weep with sorrow; / encourage me by your word.
> ☐ *When I weep with sorrow I ask the Lord to encourage me by His word.*

²⁹Keep me from lying to myself; / give me the privilege of knowing your instructions.
> ☐ *I ask the Lord to keep me from lying to myself because I want the privilege of knowing His instructions.*

³⁰I have chosen to be faithful; / I have determined to live by your regulations.
> ☐ *I am faithful and determined to live by the Lord's regulations.*

³¹I cling to your laws. / Lord, don't let me be put to shame!
> ☐ *I cling to the laws of the Lord. I ask the Lord to not let me be put to shame.*

³²I will pursue your commands, / for you expand my understanding.
> ☐ *I pursue the commands of the Lord because He expands my understanding.*

He (ה)

³³Teach me your decrees, O Lord; / I will keep them to the end.
- [ ] *I ask the Lord to teach me His decrees. I will follow the Lord's decrees to the end.*

³⁴Give me understanding and I will obey your instructions; / I will put them into practice with all my heart.
- [ ] *I ask the Lord to give me understanding so I can obey His instructions. I put His instructions into practice with all my heart.*

³⁵Make me walk along the path of your commands, / for that is where my happiness is found.
- [ ] *I ask the Lord to make me walk along the path of His commands because I know that is where my happiness is found.*

³⁶Give me an eagerness for your laws / rather than a love for money!
- [ ] *I ask the Lord to give me an eagerness for His laws rather than a love for money.*

³⁷Turn my eyes from worthless things, / and give me life through your word.
- [ ] *I ask the Lord to turn my eyes from worthless things, and give me life through His word.*

³⁸Reassure me of your promise, / made to those who fear you.
- [ ] *I ask the Lord to reassure me of His promises because I fear Him.*

³⁹Help me abandon my shameful ways; / for your regulations are good.
- [ ] *I ask the Lord to help me abandon my shameful ways because I know His regulations are good.*

⁴⁰I long to obey your commandments! / Renew my life with your goodness.
- [ ] *I long to obey the Lord's commandments. I ask the Lord to renew my life with His goodness.*

Waw (ו)

⁴¹Lord, give me your unfailing love, / the salvation that you promised me.
- [ ] *I ask the Lord to give me His unfailing love and the salvation that He promised me.*

⁴²Then I can answer those who taunt me, / for I trust in your word.
- [ ] *I trust in the Lord and His word to provide answers in difficult situations.*

⁴³Do not snatch your word of truth from me, / for your regulations are my only hope.

☐ *I am dependent on the Lᴏʀᴅ's word of truth. I know His regulations are my only hope.*

⁴⁴I will keep on obeying your instructions / forever and ever.

☐ *I will keep on obeying the instructions of the Lᴏʀᴅ forever and ever.*

⁴⁵I will walk in freedom, / for I have devoted myself to your commandments.

☐ *I will walk in freedom because I have devoted myself to the Lᴏʀᴅ's commandments.*

⁴⁶I will speak to kings about your laws, / and I will not be ashamed.

☐ *I am not ashamed of the laws of the Lᴏʀᴅ even in the presence of those in authority over me.*

⁴⁷How I delight in your commands! / How I love them!

☐ *I delight and love the commands of the Lᴏʀᴅ.*

⁴⁸I honor and love your commands. / I meditate on your decrees.

☐ *I honor and love the commands of the Lᴏʀᴅ and I meditate on His decrees.*

Zayin (ז)

⁴⁹Remember your promise to me; / it is my only hope.

☐ *I ask the Lᴏʀᴅ to remember His promise to me because I know it is my only hope.*

⁵⁰Your promise revives me; / it comforts me in all my troubles.

☐ *The promise of the Lᴏʀᴅ revives me and comforts me in all my troubles.*

⁵¹The proud hold me in utter contempt, / but I do not turn away from your instructions.

☐ *I continue to obey the instructions of the Lᴏʀᴅ even when the proud hold me in utter contempt.*

⁵²I meditate on your age-old regulations; / O Lᴏʀᴅ, they comfort me.

☐ *I meditate on the age-old regulations of the Lᴏʀᴅ because they comfort me.*

⁵³I become furious with the wicked, / because they reject your instructions.

☐ *I am furious with the wicked because they reject the instructions of the Lᴏʀᴅ.*

⁵⁴Your decrees have been the theme of my songs / wherever I have lived.

☐ *The decrees of the Lᴏʀᴅ are central to my life wherever I am.*

⁵⁵I reflect at night on who you are, O Lᴏʀᴅ; / therefore, I obey your instructions.

☐ *At night I reflect on who the Lᴏʀᴅ is; therefore, I obey His instructions.*

⁵⁶This is how I spend my life: / obeying your commandments.
- ☐ *I spend my life obeying the commandments of the Lord.*

Heth (ה)

⁵⁷Lord, you are mine! / I promise to obey your words!
- ☐ *I have a personal relationship with the Lord. I promise to obey His words.*

⁵⁸With all my heart I want your blessings. / Be merciful as you promised.
- ☐ *I want the Lord's blessings with all my heart. I ask the Lord to be merciful to me as He promised.*

⁵⁹I pondered the direction of my life, / and I turned to follow your laws.
- ☐ *As I ponder the direction of my life, I turn to follow the laws of the Lord.*

⁶⁰I will hurry, without delay, / to obey your commands.
- ☐ *I hurry, without delay, to obey the Lord's commands.*

⁶¹Evil people try to drag me into sin, / but I am firmly anchored to your instructions.
- ☐ *I am firmly anchored to the instructions of the Lord even though evil people try to drag me into sin.*

⁶²I rise at midnight to thank you / for your just regulations.
- ☐ *I rise at midnight to thank the Lord for His just regulations.*

⁶³I am a friend to anyone who fears you— / anyone who obeys your commandments.
- ☐ *I am a friend to anyone who fears the Lord and anyone who obeys His commandments.*

⁶⁴O Lord, your unfailing love fills the earth; / teach me your decrees.
- ☐ *I ask the Lord to teach me His decrees because His unfailing love fills the earth.*

Teth (ט)

⁶⁵You have done many good things for me, Lord, / just as you promised.
- ☐ *The Lord has done many good things for me just as He promised.*

⁶⁶I believe in your commands; / now teach me good judgment and knowledge.
- ☐ *I believe in the Lord's commands and I ask Him to teach me good judgment and knowledge.*

⁶⁷I used to wander off until you disciplined me; / but now I closely follow your word.

☐ *I used to wander off until the* Lord *disciplined me; but now I closely follow His word.*

⁶⁸You are good and do only good; / teach me your decrees.

☐ *I ask the* Lord *to teach me His decrees because He is good and does only good.*

⁶⁹Arrogant people smear me with lies, / but in truth I obey your commandments with all my heart.

☐ *Even though arrogant people smear me with lies, I obey the commandments of the* Lord *with all my heart.*

⁷⁰Their hearts are dull and stupid, / but I delight in your instructions.

☐ *I delight in the instructions of the* Lord, *even when difficult people distress me.*

⁷¹My suffering was good for me, / for it taught me to pay attention to your decrees.

☐ *I can say my suffering was good for me because it taught me to pay attention to the* Lord'*s decrees.*

⁷²Your instructions are more valuable to me / than millions in gold and silver.

☐ *I value the instructions of the* Lord *more than millions in gold and silver.*

Yodh (')

⁷³You made me; you created me. / Now give me the sense to follow your commands.

☐ *I ask the* Lord *to give me the sense to follow His commands because He made and created me.*

⁷⁴May all who fear you find in me a cause for joy, / for I have put my hope in your word.

☐ *I put my hope in the word of the* Lord *and my life displays joy to those who fear the* Lord.

⁷⁵I know, O Lord, that your regulations are fair; / you disciplined me because I needed it.

☐ *I know the regulations of the* Lord *are fair, and that He disciplined me because I needed it.*

⁷⁶Now let your unfailing love comfort me, / just as you promised me, your servant.

☐ *When I am in distress I ask for the* Lord'*s unfailing love to comfort me just as He promised.*

⁷⁷Surround me with your tender mercies so I may live, / for your instructions are my delight.

☐ *I ask the LORD to surround me with His tender mercies so I may live, because I delight in His instructions.*

⁷⁸Bring disgrace upon the arrogant people who lied about me; / meanwhile, I will concentrate on your commandments.

☐ *I concentrate on the LORD's commandments, even though arrogant people have lied about me.*

⁷⁹Let me be united with all who fear you, / with those who know your laws.

☐ *My social support system is comprised of those who fear the LORD and those who know the laws of the LORD.*

⁸⁰May I be blameless in keeping your decrees; / then I will never be ashamed.

☐ *I am blameless in keeping the decrees of the LORD, and I am not ashamed.*

Kaph (כ)

⁸¹I am worn out waiting for your rescue, / but I have put my hope in your word.

☐ *When I am worn out waiting for the LORD's rescue, I put my hope in His word.*

⁸²My eyes are straining to see your promises come true. / When will you comfort me?

☐ *Even when I cannot feel the comfort of the LORD, my eyes continue to strain to see His promises come true.*

⁸³I am shriveled like a wineskin in the smoke, / but I have not forgotten to obey your decrees.

☐ *Even when I feel like I am withering, I continue to obey the decrees of the LORD.*

⁸⁴How long must I wait? / When will you punish those who persecute me?

☐ *I ask the LORD to punish those who persecute me, even though I want to see justice immediately.*

⁸⁵These arrogant people who hate your instructions / have dug deep pits to trap me.

☐ *Arrogant people dig pits to trap me because they hate the LORD's instructions.*

⁸⁶All your commands are trustworthy. / Protect me from those who hunt me down without cause.

☐ *I ask the LORD to protect me from those who hunt me down without cause. I trust in the LORD's commands because they are trustworthy.*

87They almost finished me off, / but I refused to abandon your commandments.

☐ *I refuse to abandon the commandments of the LORD even when I am worn out from opposition.*

88In your unfailing love, spare my life; / then I can continue to obey your laws.

☐ *Because of the LORD's unfailing love, I ask Him to spare my life in the face of opposition so I can continue to obey His laws.*

Lamedh (ל)

89Your eternal word, O LORD, / stands firm in heaven.

☐ *I believe the word of the LORD is eternal and stands firm in heaven.*

90Your faithfulness extends to every generation, / as enduring as the earth you created.

☐ *I believe that the faithfulness of the LORD is as enduring as the earth He created, extending to every generation.*

91Your regulations remain true to this day, / for everything serves your plans.

☐ *I believe the regulations of the LORD are still relevant and that everything serves His plans.*

92If your instructions hadn't sustained me with joy, / I would have died in my misery.

☐ *I would die in my misery if the instructions of the LORD did not sustain me with joy.*

93I will never forget your commandments, / for by them you give me life.

☐ *I will never forget the LORD's commandments, for by them He gives me life.*

94I am yours; rescue me! / For I have worked hard at obeying your commandments.

☐ *I ask the LORD to rescue me because I am His. I work hard at obeying the commandments of the LORD.*

95Though the wicked hide along the way to kill me, / I will quietly keep my mind on your laws.

☐ *I am not distracted by the wicked that try to destroy me. I quietly keep my mind on the laws of the LORD.*

96Even perfection has its limits, / but your commands have no limit.

☐ *Perfectionism is not my goal because the commands of the LORD are my highest goal.*

Mem (מ)

⁹⁷Oh, how I love your instructions! / I think about them all day long.

☐ *I love the LORD's instructions, and I think about them all day long.*

⁹⁸Your commands make me wiser than my enemies, / for they are my constant guide.

☐ *The commands of the LORD are my constant guide. They make me wiser than my enemies.*

⁹⁹Yes, I have more insight than my teachers, / for I am always thinking of your laws.

☐ *I have more insight than my teachers because I am always thinking of the laws of the LORD.*

¹⁰⁰I am even wiser than my elders, / for I have kept your commandments.

☐ *I am even wiser than my elders, because I keep the commandments of the LORD.*

¹⁰¹I have refused to walk on any evil path, / so that I may remain obedient to your word.

☐ *I refuse to walk on any evil path, so that I may remain obedient to the word of the LORD.*

¹⁰²I haven't turned away from your regulations, / for you have taught me well.

☐ *I do not turn away from the regulations of the LORD, because He has taught me well.*

¹⁰³How sweet your words taste to me; / they are sweeter than honey.

☐ *I experience the words of the LORD as sweeter than honey.*

¹⁰⁴Your commandments give me understanding; / no wonder I hate every false way of life.

☐ *I hate every false way of life because the commandments of the LORD give me understanding.*

Nun (נ)

¹⁰⁵Your word is a lamp to guide my feet / and a light for my path.

☐ *The word of the LORD is a lamp to guide my feet and a light for my path.*

¹⁰⁶I've promised it once, and I'll promise it again: / I will obey your righteous regulations.

☐ *I promise to obey the righteous regulations of the LORD.*

[107]I have suffered much, O Lord; / restore my life again as you promised.

☐ *Even though I have suffered much, I believe the Lord will restore my life again as He promised.*

[108]Lord, accept my offering of praise, / and teach me your regulations.

☐ *I ask the Lord to accept my offering of praise and to teach me His regulations.*

[109]My life constantly hangs in the balance, / but I will not stop obeying your instructions.

☐ *Even though my life constantly hangs in the balance I will not stop obeying the instructions of the Lord.*

[110]The wicked have set their traps for me, / but I will not turn from your commandments.

☐ *I will not turn from the commandments of the Lord, even though the wicked set traps for me.*

[111]Your laws are my treasure; / they are my heart's delight.

☐ *The laws of the Lord are my treasure and my heart's delight.*

[112]I am determined to keep your decrees / to the very end.

☐ *I am determined to keep the decrees of the Lord to the very end.*

Samekh (ס)

[113]I hate those with divided loyalties, / but I love your instructions.

☐ *I hate those with divided loyalties, but I love the instructions of the Lord.*

[114]You are my refuge and my shield; / your word is my source of hope.

☐ *The Lord is my refuge and my shield; His word is my source of hope.*

[115]Get out of my life, you evil-minded people, / for I intend to obey the commands of my God.

☐ *I set boundaries with evil-minded people, because I intend to obey the commands of my God.*

[116]Lord, sustain me as you promised, that I may live! / Do not let my hope be crushed.

☐ *When I feel my hope is being crushed, I ask the Lord to sustain me as He promised, so I may live.*

[117]Sustain me, and I will be rescued; / then I will meditate continually on your decrees.

☐ *I ask the Lord to sustain me so I will be rescued; then I meditate continually on His decrees.*

¹¹⁸But you have rejected all who stray from your decrees. / They are only fooling themselves.

☐ *I do not fool myself by straying from the decrees of the LORD.*

¹¹⁹You skim off the wicked of the earth like scum; / no wonder I love to obey your laws!

☐ *I love to obey the laws of the LORD, because He skims off the wicked of the earth like scum.*

¹²⁰I tremble in fear of you; / I stand in awe of your regulations.

☐ *I tremble in fear of the LORD; I stand in awe of His regulations.*

Ayin (ע)

¹²¹Don't leave me to the mercy of my enemies, / for I have done what is just and right.

☐ *I do what is just and right, so I ask the LORD to not leave me to the mercy of my enemies.*

¹²²Please guarantee a blessing for me. / Don't let the arrogant oppress me!

☐ *I ask the LORD to guarantee a blessing for me. I also ask the LORD to not let the arrogant oppress me.*

¹²³My eyes strain to see your rescue, / to see the truth of your promise fulfilled.

☐ *My eyes strain to see the rescue of the LORD and to see the truth of His promise fulfilled.*

¹²⁴I am your servant; deal with me in unfailing love, / and teach me your decrees.

☐ *I am a servant of the LORD. I ask Him to deal with me in unfailing love and to teach me His decrees.*

¹²⁵Give discernment to me, your servant; / then I will understand your laws.

☐ *I ask the LORD to give me discernment so I will understand His laws.*

¹²⁶LORD, it is time for you to act, / for these evil people have violated your instructions.

☐ *I am confident that the LORD will punish evil people who violate His instructions.*

¹²⁷Truly, I love your commands / more than gold, even the finest gold.

☐ *I love the commands of the LORD more than gold, even the finest gold.*

¹²⁸Each of your commandments is right. / That is why I hate every false way.

☐ *I hate every false way, because each of the LORD's commandments is right.*

Pe (𝔓)

¹²⁹Your laws are wonderful. / No wonder I obey them!

☐ *I obey the L*ORD*'s laws because they are wonderful.*

¹³⁰The teaching of your word gives light, / so even the simple can understand.

☐ *The teaching of the L*ORD*'s word gives light so even I can understand.*

¹³¹I pant with expectation, / longing for your commands.

☐ *I pant with expectation, longing for the commands of the L*ORD*.*

¹³²Come and show me your mercy, / as you do for all who love your name.

☐ *I ask the L*ORD *to come and show me His mercy, as He does for all who love His name.*

¹³³Guide my steps by your word, / so I will not be overcome by evil.

☐ *I ask the L*ORD *to guide my steps by His word, so I will not be overcome by evil.*

¹³⁴Ransom me from the oppression of evil people; / then I can obey your commandments.

☐ *I ask the L*ORD *to ransom me from the oppression of evil people so that I can obey His commandments.*

¹³⁵Look upon me with love; / teach me your decrees.

☐ *I ask the L*ORD *to look upon me with love and teach me His decrees.*

¹³⁶Rivers of tears gush from my eyes / because people disobey your instructions.

☐ *Rivers of tears gush from my eyes because people disobey the instructions of the L*ORD*.*

Tsadhe (𝔗)

¹³⁷O L*ORD*, you are righteous, / and your regulations are fair.

☐ *I believe the L*ORD *is righteous and all His regulations are fair.*

¹³⁸Your laws are perfect / and completely trustworthy.

☐ *I believe the laws of the L*ORD *are perfect and completely trustworthy.*

¹³⁹I am overwhelmed with indignation, / for my enemies have disregarded your words.

☐ *I am overwhelmed with anger because my enemies have disregarded the words of the L*ORD*.*

¹⁴⁰Your promises have been thoroughly tested; / that is why I love them so much.

☐ *I love the promises of the L*ORD*, because I know they are valid.*

¹⁴¹I am insignificant and despised, / but I don't forget your commandments.

   ☐ *Even when I feel insignificant and despised I do not forget the commandments of the Lord.*

¹⁴²Your justice is eternal, / and your instructions are perfectly true.

   ☐ *I believe the justice of the Lord is eternal and His instructions are perfectly true.*

¹⁴³As pressure and stress bear down on me, / I find joy in your commands.

   ☐ *As pressure and stress bear down on me, I find joy in the commands of the Lord.*

¹⁴⁴Your laws are always right; / help me to understand them so I may live.

   ☐ *I know the Lord's laws are always right. I ask the Lord to help me understand His laws so I may live.*

Qoph (ק)

¹⁴⁵I pray with all my heart; answer me, Lord! / I will obey your decrees.

   ☐ *I pray with all my heart for the Lord to answer me. I will obey His decrees.*

¹⁴⁶I cry out to you; rescue me, / that I may obey your laws.

   ☐ *I cry out to the Lord to rescue me so that I may obey His laws.*

¹⁴⁷I rise early, before the sun is up; / I cry out for help and put my hope in your words.

   ☐ *I rise early, before the sun is up; I cry out for help and put my hope in the words of the Lord.*

¹⁴⁸I stay awake through the night, / thinking about your promise.

   ☐ *I stay awake through the night thinking about the Lord's promise.*

¹⁴⁹In your faithful love, O Lord, hear my cry; / let me be revived by following your regulations.

   ☐ *I ask the Lord in His faithful love to hear my cry and let me be revived by following His regulations.*

¹⁵⁰Lawless people are coming to attack me; / they live far from your instructions.

   ☐ *I trust the Lord even when lawless people are coming to attack me, because they live far from the Lord's instructions.*

¹⁵¹But you are near, O Lord, / and all your commands are true.

   ☐ *I believe the Lord is near and all His commands are true.*

¹⁵²I have known from my earliest days / that your laws will last forever.

   ☐ *I have known from my earliest days that the laws of the Lord will last forever.*

Resh (ר)

¹⁵³Look upon my suffering and rescue me, / for I have not forgotten your instructions.

☐ *I do not forget the instructions of the* Lord *even when I am suffering and I ask Him to rescue me.*

¹⁵⁴Argue my case; take my side! / Protect my life as you promised.

☐ *I ask the* Lord *to argue my case, take my side and to protect my life as He promised.*

¹⁵⁵The wicked are far from rescue, / for they do not bother with your decrees.

☐ *I believe the wicked cannot be rescued, because they do not bother with the decrees of the* Lord.

¹⁵⁶Lord, how great is your mercy; / let me be revived by following your regulations.

☐ *I praise the* Lord *for His great mercy and I ask Him to let me be revived by following His regulations.*

¹⁵⁷Many persecute and trouble me, / yet I have not swerved from your laws.

☐ *I do not swerve from the laws of the* Lord, *even though many people persecute and trouble me.*

¹⁵⁸Seeing these traitors makes me sick at heart, / because they care nothing for your word.

☐ *I am sick at heart when I see traitors, because they do not care for the word of the* Lord.

¹⁵⁹See how I love your commandments, Lord. / Give back my life because of your unfailing love.

☐ *I ask the* Lord *to give back my life because of His unfailing love and because it is evident how much I love His commandments.*

¹⁶⁰The very essence of your words is truth; / all your just regulations will stand forever.

☐ *I believe the very essence of the* Lord's *words is truth and that all His just regulations will stand forever.*

Shin (ש)

¹⁶¹Powerful people harass me without cause, / but my heart trembles only at your word.

☐ *Powerful people may harass me without cause, but my heart trembles only at the word of the* Lord.

¹⁶²I rejoice in your word / like one who discovers a great treasure.

☐ *I rejoice in the word of the* LORD *like one who discovers a great treasure.*

¹⁶³I hate and abhor all falsehood, / but I love your instructions.

☐ *I hate and abhor all falsehood, but I love the instructions of the* LORD.

¹⁶⁴I will praise you seven times a day / because all your regulations are just.

☐ *I will praise the* LORD *seven times a day because all His regulations are just.*

¹⁶⁵Those who love your instructions have great peace / and do not stumble.

☐ *I have great peace and do not stumble, because I love the instructions of the* LORD.

¹⁶⁶I long for your rescue, LORD, / so I have obeyed your commands.

☐ *I long for the* LORD's *rescue, so I have obeyed His commands.*

¹⁶⁷I have obeyed your laws, / for I love them very much.

☐ *I obey the laws of the* LORD *because I love them very much.*

¹⁶⁸Yes, I obey your commandments and laws / because you know everything I do.

☐ *I obey the commandments and laws of the* LORD, *because He knows everything I do.*

Taw (ת)

¹⁶⁹O LORD, listen to my cry; / give me the discerning mind you promised.

☐ *I ask the* LORD *to listen to my cry and give me the discerning mind that He promised.*

¹⁷⁰Listen to my prayer; / rescue me as you promised.

☐ *I ask the* LORD *to listen to my prayer and rescue me as He promised.*

¹⁷¹Let praise flow from my lips, / for you have taught me your decrees.

☐ *Praise flows from my lips, because the* LORD *has taught me His decrees.*

¹⁷²Let my tongue sing about your word, / for all your commands are right.

☐ *I sing about the word of the* LORD, *because all His commands are right.*

¹⁷³Give me a helping hand, / for I have chosen to follow your commandments.

☐ *I ask the* LORD *for a helping hand, because I have chosen to follow His commandments.*

¹⁷⁴O LORD, I have longed for your rescue, / and your instructions are my delight.

☐ *I long for the rescue of the* LORD, *because His instructions are my delight.*

¹⁷⁵Let me live so I can praise you, / and may your regulations help me.

☐ *I ask the* LORD *to let me live so I can praise Him, and for His regulations to help me.*

[176]I have wandered away like a lost sheep; / come and find me, / for I have not forgotten your commands.

☐ *Even though I have wandered away like a lost sheep, I ask the* LORD *to come find me because I have not forgotten His commands.*

Whew! Did you really read the whole psalm and evaluate each personalization statement, or did you just skip here to see what comes next? Maybe we should subtract some points for skipping!

The German word *langweilig* has frequently come to mind as I (Melanie) have worked through Psalm 119. The German/English dictionary translates the word as "tedious, wearisome, tiresome,"[2] but that still doesn't convey the idea for me. Boring definitely doesn't cut it either. But if you were to make the trip from Tennessee to China, the process would be *langweilig*. If you were looking for a needle in a jar of pins, that chore would be *langweilig*. Suppose you are preparing to move from your home of twenty-five years—that would be *langweilig*. Each of these examples has its rewards at the completion of the process, but the process itself is *langweilig*.

The overriding question throughout this *langweilig* exercise is to determine, "Am I desperately dependent in my relationship with the Lord, or do I continue in my independence from Him?" As I am striving to find Him relevant to every area of my life, these verses serve as a reminder of how He is relevant to my relationship responses, my thought life, my joys, my sorrows, my prayers, my praise, my standards, and my survival.

You may have noticed some patterns as you traveled the path of Psalm 119. For example, the multiplicity of personalization phrases containing the word *ask* points to the condition of your prayer life. The personalization phrases that use the word *believe* indicate your convictions and understanding that results in the application of specific truth. Did you mark only verses that offer you a personal reward? Did you check all the verses that indicated dire circumstances? Did you select the passages you thought a significant person in your life would approve?

Perhaps you have realized as you proceeded through this exercise that you are incapable of arriving at the various milestones. Yay, God! That is the point! In and of yourself you are powerless to accomplish His purposes in your life! It is only through His divine enablement that we can be personally empowered to live as Christ lived and desires us to live. Remember, God has supplied everything that is necessary for life and godliness, but we must allow Him to accomplish His purposes in our lives.

How did you do? Count all your marks.

"I marked _____ of the 176 verses."

Now prayerfully consider which category authentically describes you *currently* and *consistently*. Of course, these are not hard and concrete determinations, because we are humans who are prone to error and deception that may cause us to evaluate ourselves either better or worse than God sees us. But the following continuum can offer a basic understanding of the status of your relationship with God and the direction you are heading.

☐ **Independent of God**—I am resistant to God working in my life. I want to be the captain of my own ship and determine my own direction. I am actually a very dependent person, but not dependent on God.

☐ **Searching for God**—I recognize I have a need for God in my life. I'm not doing so well at making it on my own. I am looking for solutions in my life and think God may be the answer. But I choose people, positions, and possessions to fill the God place in my life.

☐ **Desiring God**—I want to have a relationship with God, so I am attempting to satisfy that yearning. I think I know what God wants, and I want what God wants, so I pray and ask for mercy and deliverance, but return to my sins soon after. I find myself desperate, but not desperately dependent on God. I want to be dependent, but I'm just not there. I'm set on doing it my way.

☐ **Connecting with God**—I have a union with God that offers me fellowship. But I also have trust issues that result in fear and make me wonder, "If I turn everything over, what will happen?" I still have a long way to go, but I think I am on the right track. I am easily distracted from God's purpose, but I am learning that He is faithful and continuously pulling me back to Him. I am learning to depend on Him only.

☐ **Desperately dependent on God**—I am not perfect, but I have an unwavering trust that He is the best and only option for navigating this life. He knows what is necessary for me, so I rely on His divine enablement for my personal empowerment as I pursue my greatest goal of glorifying Him. (If you believe you fall in this category, prayerfully consider if you actually completed the exercise honestly, or if you were merely choosing what you want to be true of you.)

If you are really brave and want to know more about yourself, you might consider asking someone close to you to complete the Evaluation of Desperate Dependency with you in mind. God does place people in our lives to assist us in our growth process. But if you are resistant to another's assessment and feedback, there is the potential that your relationship will be scarred as a result. However, if someone completes the exercise on your behalf, your relationship may be strengthened because of the authentication of their commitment to your maturity.

Insight Journal

1. What has God shown you about yourself through this evaluation?
2. What has God revealed about Himself through this assessment?
3. How will you respond to the insight you have gained?

Endnotes

Chapter 1

1. James Dobson, *Solid Answers* (Wheaton, IL: Tyndale, 1997), 105–106.

Chapter 2

1. *Merriam-Webster® Online Dictionary*, s.v. "independent," http://www.merriam-webster.com/dictionary/independent (accessed January 26, 2010).
2. *Merriam-Webster® Online Dictionary*, s.v. "dependent," http://www.merriam-webster.com/dictionary/dependent (accessed January 26, 2010).

Chapter 3

1. *Merriam-Webster® Online Dictionary*, s.v. "manipulate," http://www.merriam-webster.com/dictionary/manipulate (accessed January 26, 2010).

Chapter 5

1. Neil Anderson, *Victory over the Darkness* (Ventura, CA: Regal Books, 2000), 161.
2. Michael Easley, *Proclaim!* aired on WMBW February 2, 2008.

Chapter 6

1. *Merriam-Webster® Online Dictionary*, s.v. "relevant," http://www.merriam-webster.com/dictionary/relevant (accessed January 26, 2010).

Chapter 8

1. *Merriam-Webster® Online Dictionary*, s.v. "jealous," http://www.merriam-webster.com/dictionary/jealous (accessed February 20, 2010).

Chapter 9

1. *Merriam-Webster® Online Dictionary*, s.v. "forgive," http://www.merriam-webster.com/dictionary/forgive (accessed January 25, 2010).

Chapter 10

1. James Strong, *The Exhaustive Concordance of the Bible* (electronic ed.; Ontario: Woodside Bible Fellowship, 1996), G25.
2. Strong, *Concordance*, G1391.
3. Gerhard Kittel, et al., eds., *Theological Dictionary of the New Testament* (electronic ed.; Grand Rapids, MI: Eerdmans, 1964–c1976), 6:870.
4. C. S. Lewis, *Mere Christianity* (New York: HarperCollins, 2001), 227.

Appendix D

1. Warren W. Wiersbe, *Wiersbe's Expository Outlines on the Old Testament* (Wheaton, IL: Victor Books, 1993), Ps 119:1.
2. "langweilig,"*A New German/English Dictionary for General Use* (New York: David McKay, 1930), 492.

Contact Information

To order additional copies of this book, please visit
www.redemption-press.com.
Also available on Amazon.com and BarnesandNoble.com
Or by calling toll free 1-844-2REDEEM.

CPSIA information can be obtained at www.ICGtesting.com
Printed in the USA
LVOW03s0608161014

408948LV00003B/6/P